14

THE ADMINISTRATION OF UNITED KINGDOM FOREIGN POLICY THROUGH THE UNITED NATIONS

THE ADMINISTRATION OF UNITED KINGDOM FOREIGN POLICY THROUGH THE UNITED NATIONS

by

ROSALYN HIGGINS

edited by **Gerard J. Mangone**

THE MAXWELL SCHOOL OF CITIZENSHIP
AND PUBLIC AFFAIRS
SYRACUSE UNIVERSITY, SYRACUSE, NEW YORK

Rosalyn Higgins is a member of the research staff of Chatham House. She read law at the Universities of Cambridge and Yale, and in 1958 was the United Kingdom intern at the United Nations. From 1959-1961 she was Commonwealth Fund Fellow at the Law School, Yale University, and in 1960 was a Visiting Fellow at the Brookings Institution, Washington. From 1961 to the end of September 1963 she was a Junior Fellow in International Studies at the London School of Economics. She is the author of *The Development of International Law Through the Political Organs of the United Nations* and *Conflict of Interests: International Law in a Divided World*.

Gerard J. Mangone is Associate Dean of the Maxwell School of Citizenship and Public Affairs at Syracuse University and Director of the International Relations Program.

Preface

This is the first of a series of studies on the administration of foreign policy through the United Nations by a number of governments in the contemporary international system.

Both scholars and statesmen have recognized for some time the impact that the United Nations system is having upon traditional diplomacy, but little research thus far has been directed toward the administrative changes within national governments to accommodate mid-twentieth century practices in multilateral peacekeeping, economic assistance, and social cooperation.

Rosalyn Higgins, who is a member of the research staff of Chatham House, describes in this book the organization of the United Kingdom government for carrying out its foreign policies through the United Nations and the specialized agencies. She indicates the allocation of responsibilities for the UN system in the various British ministries, the role of the permanent delegations in New York and Geneva, some problems of staffing and program coordination, and the part that Parliament and the public play in influencing the government on issues touching the United Nations.

The manuscript was originally presented at the Second Maxwell Institute on the United Nations in August, 1965 at the Villa Serbelloni of the Rockefeller Foundation at Bellagio, Italy. Twenty members of the Institute, from eleven different countries, all with academic and government experience in United Nations affairs, reviewed and discussed the essay, which was then revised and finally edited at the Maxwell School of Syracuse University.

Syracuse, New York   — Gerard J. Mangone
February, 1966

The Administration of United Kingdom Foreign Policy Through the United Nations

The British Commitment to International Organization

The rapid evolution of new states in the international system, the growing interdependence of nations in the economic sphere, and the constantly changing technical and military knowledge of our world are all factors that profoundly affect the contemporary foreign policy of the United Kingdom. In order that policy may keep pace with events, an efficient administration of foreign affairs must match the new international needs.

A modern foreign policy must take cognizance of the existence of a large body of international organizations, especially the United Nations system. Like other governments, the United Kingdom today is required to ponder new problems, to provide information, to organize delegations, and to participate in a myriad of international activities. The United Nations is available as an instrument of diplomacy and as a forum for promoting British views. Equally, the public defense of national policy may be taken to that forum while decisions may be made by the United Nations that affect the national interest. Above all, for its members the United Nations means a commitment to multilateral diplomacy.

This study emphasizes the present and recent past,[1] particularly the methods and techniques by which membership in the UN is transformed into foreign policy. The substance and administration of foreign policy are, of course, inseparably intertwined: the one reflects the

---

[1]An indication of the measure of change between 1945 and 1965 in the administration of UN policy may be seen by consulting Max Beloff, *New Dimensions in Foreign Policy: A Study in British Administration Experience, 1947-1959*, New York, Macmillan Co., 1961 and D. N. Chester and F. M. G. Willson, *The Organization of British Central Government, 1914-56*, London, Allen and Unwin, 1957.

other. Changes in government administration thus indicate not only the growing complexity of international affairs, but also the varying fortunes of the United Kingdom at the UN and her attitude to the organization.

Great Britain's role in the United Nations has always been a significant one: a founder member, and one of the Big Five, a nation with a long diplomatic history, she has been well disposed towards the UN. She has sought to strengthen the authority of the Secretariat and generally supported the peace-keeping functions of the Organization. She has participated willingly in the economic and social activities of the UN, and though she has generally sought to keep the overall budgets down she has always paid her assessments promptly, as well as contributing to the several voluntary programs. Britain has provided distinguished servants for the UN and has had a special role not only as a permanent member, but also as a leader of the Commonwealth, a close ally of the United States, and an important European nation.

The United Kingdom's support, therefore, for the basic idea of international organization cannot be doubted. At the same time, two experiences have undoubtedly affected the British attitude towards the UN: Suez and the process of decolonization. At the time of Suez a part of the British public and, of course, the government saw the UN as an instrument of humiliation. The abrupt realization of the limits of British power coincided with the emergence of a strengthened role for the UN and the experience inevitably left some psychological scars, which have generally been exaggerated. A more prolonged effect upon Britain has been the need felt to adopt a defensive posture in the face of UN demands about the scope and speed of the decolonizing process. Reasonable requests from the UN have been mixed with unreasonable ones, but in both Britain has often felt herself under attack. Welcome signs are now emerging that this period of strained relations between the United Kingdom and the UN may be soon past, leaving still the problem of formulating the United Kingdom's policy for today and tomorrow.

Government Structure and the United Nations

The formulation and presentation of United Kingdom policy in the UN is, of course, a part of the conduct of foreign affairs. Control of the conduct of foreign relations is the prerogative of the Crown as represented by the Government. Diplomatic negotiations may take place and officials may be appointed without particular reference to Parliament. At the same time, the Government cannot survive without a majority in the House of Commons, which means control of that

2

House. Although the power of the Government in the field of foreign affairs, including the UN, is strong, Parliament may, by various techniques, extract a certain amount of information from the Government and require it to be mindful of the ever-present need for a majority on important issues.

The Prime Minister is the leader of the party that either has the majority of seats or in coalition can maintain a majority in the House of Commons. He selects his ministers, some of whom become ministers of Cabinet rank, some not; but there exists a strong doctrine of collective Cabinet responsibility. Once a decision relating to the UN has become British policy, the Cabinet is collectively responsible for it. Conflicts between different ministerial departments on any UN question will thus, if necessary, have to be settled at ministerial level. Each of the Cabinet ranking ministers is head of his own ministry, and there may also be junior ministers serving beneath him within that ministry. His officials are entirely non-political appointments and will be mainly permanent career civil servants. The senior Foreign Office posts do not, therefore, change with the change of government and the civil service continues to serve whichever Government happens to be in power. This makes for both continuity and stability, but it probably makes departures in policy more difficult for an incoming Government than it anticipates. The facilities and knowledge at the disposal of the civil service machine puts it in a powerful position vis a vis its political ministers. Nonetheless, a strong minister can insist upon what he will within his own department, and if he is adamant and persistent, his civil servants will, of course, obey and service the needs of the new policy. This applies to UN policy as much as to any other aspect of foreign affairs. These general observations must not be taken to imply either that the civil service is always against change in policy or that, on those occasions where they urge no change, they are necessarily wrong.

When the Labour government was returned to office in the United Kingdom in October, 1964, after thirteen years in opposition, a cluster of new departments were established in Whitehall and there was a considerable reallocation of work. From the point of view of the UN, the establishment of a new Ministry for Overseas Development was of major significance, and so was the appointment of a United Kingdom representative at the UN of ministerial rank. These will be described later, but such changes have inevitably caused certain resentments among some people as well as approval by others, with a continuing debate between ministries and between individuals, in muted tones, on the proper pattern of administration of British policy in the UN and its agencies.

3

The main responsibility for relations between the United Kingdom and the UN lies with the Foreign Office. But other departments have a keen interest in them, especially with respect to policy in the UN specialized agencies. The Ministry of Overseas Development, for example, is concerned with foreign economic aid, the Board of Trade with UNCTAD* and IMCO, the Ministry of Aviation with ICAO, the Ministry of Labour with ILO, the Ministry of Health with WHO, and so on. The issue thus arises, not only which ministries should have responsibility for which particular aspects of UN work, but also how far, and by what means, should attempts be made to standardize United Kingdom practice in the various UN bodies? Once standardization is attempted, one is immediately faced with the question of the criteria to be applied. To put it in its most crude form, will the case for consistent political attitudes in the specialized agencies prove stronger than arguments in favor of functional pragmatism?

The Foreign Office has recently shown a preference for standardizing United Kingdom policy in the specialized agencies on the grounds that to do so makes political and administrative sense, with some attempt to coordinate United Kingdom policy in the specialized agencies with British allies. In much of the reallocation of responsibility for relationships with specialized agencies within Whitehall, the Government has believed that the political and administrative questions are as important in these multilateral bodies as the purely technical aspects of their work.

In 1946 a Steering Committee on International Organization (IOC) was set up at Whitehall to coordinate policies being presented before the different international organizations. The chairmanship has been given to the Foreign Office and the members of the Committee are senior officials in various interested Ministries. The IOC used to be serviced by the Cabinet Office, but it now has no official secretariat and is serviced by the Foreign Office. Much of its work has been delegated to committees or working parties, and because of the slowness involved, the IOC is today little used for any policy making functions. To arrive at a decision on a particular point, it is rarely necessary to consult a wide range of ministries represented on the IOC, for it is simpler to deal with the three or four men involved. On policy formulation on broad issues, other committees have been found more appropriate. The main function of the IOC, therefore, is as a clearing house for information. It provides a standard method for the distribution of documents among fourteen or fifteen ministries, and is a convenient focusing point for reports on concluded conferences and

---

*For a list of United Nations abbreviations used in this book, see page 62.

4

meetings of international organizations. It meets *ad hoc,* and what was once the central coordinating machinery for UN questions is now one thread in a web of interwoven committees.

The Foreign Office

The United Nations Departments. The Foreign Office itself has two UN departments, one to deal with the political aspects of UN policy and the other to deal with the economic and social aspects. It is in the Foreign Office that overall responsibility rests for United Kingdom policy in the UN. Notwithstanding all the various functional interests of other ministries, the projection of British policy in international organizations is, of course, a question of foreign policy. The chain of command is clear enough: the heads of the two UN departments in the Foreign Office are responsible to the same under secretary: and he is in this field the most senior civil servant. The under secretary is responsible to the Minister of State at the Foreign Office who is concerned with the UN.[2] He in turn is responsible to the Secretary of State for Foreign Affairs, who must retain the confidence of the Prime Minister. The Secretary of State for Foreign Affairs or, when he so designates, his Minister of State, speaks for the Foreign Office in Parliament and must there answer any questions on the United Kingdom policy in the UN.

After the Labour Government was returned to office in October 1964, a new departure occurred which is directly relevant to British policy-making for the UN. In addition to the former two ministers of state of the Foreign Office, two new ministers of state for Foreign Affairs were appointed. The first of these, Lord Chalfont, was entrusted with disarmament, while the second, Lord Caradon, formerly Hugh Foot, was appointed as the United Kingdom Permanent Representative to the United Nations. It was the first time that the leader of the British mission had been a Minister of State, that is to say, a political appointment, rather than a senior civil servant. None of the four ministers of state had Cabinet rank, but the appointment of Lord Caradon may be read as a deliberate attempt to upgrade the importance of the UN in United Kingdom policy thinking. Given Hugh Foot's personal history and experience at the UN, the appointment showed the United Kingdom as a supporter of the UN, although it in no way reflected dissatisfaction with the previous leadership of the United Kingdom mission at the official level, nor did it imply that the recommendations of the officials had failed to carry weight. The creation of a Minister

---

[2] Of the four ministers of state at the Foreign Office in 1965, George Thompson was responsible for UN affairs.

of State to lead the United Kingdom mission may well be regarded as an endeavour to give higher priority to the UN in the formulation and practice of British foreign policy.

After Lord Caradon's appointment, there were no major departures from previously established policy at the United Nations, though differences of presentation and style could undoubtedly be discerned. Certain welcome initiatives were taken in 1965, not involving any radical departures from previous policy, but indicating a desire to take certain initiatives to support the UN, such as the earmarking of logistical support for six battalions for UN use and the allocation of $10,000,000 as a voluntary contribution to the UN expenses. Such initiatives were the result of common endeavours by the United Kingdom representative at the UN, the Minister of State at the Foreign Office concerned with UN affairs, the senior civil servants, and the Foreign Secretary. It is perhaps overstating the case to say that the ideas of the United Kingdom representative at the UN carry more weight if he is a Minister of State than if he is a civil servant: in the higher echelons of policy-making personality and ability are ultimately more significant than mere formal title or rank. The minister at the head of the mission does not confine himself to matters of procedure and style, but plays an active — and sometimes initiating — role in suggestions on policy. Although *decisions* on suggested policy remain with the Foreign Office, the ministry finds itself responding to proposals from New York as well as acting on its own.

There has also been an attempt, in the formulation of policy on UN matters, to make more use of expert opinion from outside the government. To this end, an "expert panel" of private individuals was appointed to advise Lord Caradon on issues affecting the UN, an innovation admirable in principle, but something less than a success: some of the panelists appear to have been chosen for their general eminence rather than for their knowledge of the UN; while the knowledge of others relates more to the early history of the UN than to contemporary matters and the group as a whole has found that difficulties arose from the prolonged absences abroad of Lord Caradon himself. The intervening weeks between meetings were not used for any serious study or report-preparation by the panelists and no work in depth was thus being prepared, outside the civil service, for the United Kingdom representative at the UN. At the same time, the very convening of the panel has encouraged certain issues to be talked through, on a wide basis and has provided very useful contacts for officials and non-officials alike.

It is the Foreign Office UN (Political) Department which has responsibility for general UN policy; the tendering of advice to other departments; the application of the Charter; machinery and procedure; relations with the UN Secretariat; international security under the Charter; and general political questions. The Whitehall IOC also falls formally within its province.

All telegrams from the UN and concerning the UN come daily upon the desk of the head of the UN (Political) Department, while the head of the UN (Economic and Social) Department receives the telegrams relating to his responsibilities. Equally, the Foreign Office is the official channel of communication for the permanent missions in New York and Geneva, and indeed for all delegations to the UN family of agencies — even if particular delegations are led from other ministries. A large part of the day-to-day decision-making on UN matters falls to the head of the UN (Political) Department; he will, upon his own discretion, go to his Under Secretary for advice and consultation upon any matters that involve a change in policy or major decisions upon newly arising questions. On difficult problems, discussions will take place between the heads of the UN departments, the under secretary, the Minister of State, the Legal Adviser, and, if necessary, the Secretary of State himself. Any notable difference of opinion between, for example, Foreign Office officials and the United Kingdom representative at the UN would be resolved by the Secretary of State for Foreign Affairs. The role of the Legal Adviser will be examined later, but it suffices to say for the moment, that within the Foreign Office UN departments, each UN specialized agency is assigned a particular counsellor from the Legal Adviser's staff, while the Legal Adviser himself offers advice on UN matters to the head of the UN (Political) Department.

The Foreign Office itself is divided into geographical and subject departments, and the head of the UN (Political) Department consults frequently with geographical departments. Thus on Arab-Israel questions within the UN framework, the Foreign Office UN departments have been in close touch with the Foreign Office geographical departments involved. There are a range of issues which involve consultations not only between geographical and subject divisions within the Foreign Office, but also between ministries. In the handling of the Southern Rhodesia question in the UN, for example, there was, of course, close consultation between the Foreign Office and the Commonwealth Relations Office, with general policy lead by the Commonwealth Relations Office. UN matters relating to dependent territories — trusteeship or otherwise — usually calls for consultation between the Colonial Office and the Foreign Office. The handling of the Aden issue in the UN Special Committee of 24, for illustration, necessitated cooperation between the International Relations Department of the Colonial Office,

7

the UN departments, and the Arabian Department of the Foreign Office. Coordination between the Colonial Office, the Foreign Office, and the Commonwealth Relations Office for the trusteeship of Nauru is required because the territory is administered jointly with Australia and New Zealand.

By far the greater part of this coordination is done informally: within the Foreign Office, minutes are exchanged, informal visits paid, and phone calls made. The relationship between the Foreign Office and the Commonwealth Relations Office is much the same, for they are both housed in the same building, and there has been an increasing tendency to integration, as will be indicated later. On the political side of UN policy, speed is frequently essential, so that the obligatory use of a standing committee structure for coordination would be inappropriate. The same emphasis on speed does not usually hold with respect to UN economic and social matters, and here inter-ministry coordination is carried out by use of committees as well as *ad hoc*, while any new Government can be expected to set up transient inter-ministry committees to re-examine United Kingdom attitudes towards particular aspects of UN policy.

In all these matters personalities will frequently count more than coordinative techniques or formal chains of command. Personal friendships obviously exist between persons in different ministries and departments while particular officials have the ear of particular ministers. Moreover, persons outside of the formal channel of authority frequently have access to certain ministers and play their role in policy-formation.[3]

The second of the two Foreign Office UN departments deals basically with all the economic and social aspects of the UN, though the establishment of the new Ministry of Overseas Development has reduced its role in aid and development to one of coordination. The head of the UN (Economic and Social) Department is responsible to the same Under Secretary as the head of the UN (Political) Department. The social side of its work includes such matters as refugees, human rights, and narcotics control.

This Department receives the advance notice of the Economic and Social Council agenda as well as the Second (Economic Affairs) and Third (Social Affairs) Committees of the General Assembly. Decisions are made here on the assignment of the briefs, with the majority of them done within the Foreign Office itself. The Ministry of Overseas

---

[3]For studies of British pressure groups on foreign policy, see U. D. Stewart, *British Pressure Groups, Their Role in Relation to the House of Commons,* Oxford, Clarendon Press, 1958; Ian Waller, "Pressure Politics," in *Encounter,* Vol. XIX, No. 2, August, 1962; and Max Beloff, "Beyond Pressure Politics," *Encounter,* Vol. XIX, No. 5, November, 1962.

Development, however, has responsibility for those relating specifically to aid and technical assistance. All departments have worked toward a June 20th deadline for a June 30th opening of ECOSOC. Informal drafts, meanwhile, are exchanged with other ministries, and informal agreement reached, with some use made of the IOC for distribution purposes. Any major new departures in policy go up to the minister for approval, and the minister will also be consulted about major speeches.

Since the minister at the United Nations may of necessity be abroad for prolonged periods, a close working relationship develops between the heads of the two UN departments, the under secretary, and the Minister of State at the Foreign Office who is responsible for UN affairs. Where the minister has a strong personal interest in the UN, the relationship can be a most fruitful one.

The delegation to the main annual meeting of ECOSOC at Geneva in 1965 was led by the United Kingdom Permanent Representative to the UN, Lord Caradon, although he did not stay for the entire meeting. The official leader was Sir Keith Unwin who was in charge of all economic and social matters in the permanent mission in New York and who was attended by three or four other professional staff who worked with him in New York. The Minister for Overseas Development was briefly a member of the delegation and made a speech, but no one else from that ministry attended. The small permanent mission to the European office of the UN at Geneva also contributed to the delegation and it has been normal for the head of the UN (Economic and Social) Department or his deputy to attend, as well as representatives from the Ministry of Overseas Development and the Treasury.

Although the permanent mission in Geneva handles liaison work with WHO and ILO, overall responsibility for the UN specialized agencies still lies with the Foreign Office, except that UNESCO and FAO are now dealt with by the Ministry of Overseas Development, which will be described later.

Although the Overseas Development Ministry or the functional ministry will usually lead the delegates to the specialized agencies, the Foreign Office is represented through the permanent mission in Geneva or through the local British Embassy. Although the Overseas Development Ministry is now responsible for development aid, other social and economic aspects of UN work remain in the Foreign Office: thus the Foreign Office still decides the United Kingdom contribution to refugee relief and possibly the contribution to the new UN Research and Training Institute. The UN (Economic and Social) Department also played an important role in the United Nations Conference on Trade and Development which was held before the Overseas Development Min-

9

istry had been created, although the Board of Trade provided the ministerial leader and now has prime responsibility in the UN Trade and Development Board. The Foreign Office, however, provided the senior official at the UNCTAD negotiations and close links with the Board of Trade continue to be maintained. On the economic and social side, coordination also occurs at a formal level through various Cabinet committees, ministerial committees, and official committees, while any aspect of UN work that cuts across the responsibilities of several departments will often lead to a special Whitehall committee.

The regional commissions of ECOSOC also fall within the scope of the Overseas Development Ministry. Although ECA was previously handled in the Foreign Office African Department, ECLA in the American Department, and the ECAFE in the Far East Department, it is now the UN (Economic and Social) Department which is the main Foreign Office contact for all of these, while the main responsibility for them has been transferred to the Overseas Development Ministry. ECA, it should be added, remains in its entirety within the Foreign Office, though within the Economic Relations Department rather than the UN Department. Since the ECE has not to any degree been concerned with aid functions, there has been no logical reason to transfer it to the Overseas Development Ministry.

The Atomic Energy and Disarmament Department. The Atomic Energy and Disarmament Department in the Foreign Office formulates policy on the military aspects of atomic energy, and on conventional and atomic disarmament. It is involved in the multilateral disarmament discussions under the auspices of the UN in the Disarmament Commission and the negotiations at Geneva which are reported to the UN. This department is in the unusual position of having a minister in the Foreign Office responsible specifically for the area in which it works and this uncommon position gives rise to a very close relationship between the minister concerned and the head of the department. The head of the department will, in fact, show most things to the minister's private secretary, for information, even if no ministerial decision is required. Lord Chalfont, who was appointed to the new post of Minister of State with special responsibility for Disarmament by the Labour Government in 1965, was like all the ministers of state in the Foreign Office, responsible to the Foreign Secretary. The senior civil servant responsible to Lord Chalfont in the field of disarmament was one of the deputy undersecretaries. At the same level, there was a deputy under secretary responsible, among other things, for Atomic Energy. The head of the Atomic Energy and Disarmament Department was responsible to both of these.

Briefs for ministers, for conferences, statements of the Government's position, are all handled from this department, but the question of how the United Kingdom should vote, however, either in New York or in Geneva has nearly always gone to a minister for decision, either to the Minister of State for Disarmament, or, if he is away, to the Foreign Secretary.

The department has also dealt with the military aspects of outer space. Other outer space problems, as well as the peaceful aspects of atomic energy, fall to the Scientific Relations Department of the Foreign Office. The Atomic Energy and Disarmament Department has a strong coordinative function, which it performs ad hoc rather than through the IOC. Inside the Foreign Office, it has kept close links with the UN (Political) Department, since that department is responsible for current UN peacekeeping while it is concerned with long term disarmament. Although some attempts have been made to identify what is properly considered long-range or short-range, this difficulty has not been fully resolved. While the department may see all telegrams on negotiations with the UN committee of 33 for peacekeeping, for example, it has not felt it necessary to urge the UN (Political) Department to secure, in that context, any particular objectives which may have long-run implications for disarmament.

Another innovation relating to the Minister of State for Disarmament has been the establishing of a Disarmament Advisory Panel, which has set up working groups and has produced draft policy papers on such questions as the non-proliferation of atomic weapons. The department comments for the Minister on the working papers, for the Advisory Panel has no access to official documentation, and although the Advisory Panel makes a useful contribution, it is limited by lack of time, money, and access to classified material. The final paper is circulated to other interested departments in the Foreign Office and to the Ministry of Defence, and, after taking their comments into account, the head of the Atomic Energy and Disarmament Department makes recommendations to the minister.

The department, of course, deals directly with the Ministry of Defence on matters relating to the military aspects of atomic energy and disarmament and plays a significant part in policy formulation for the Geneva Conference on Disarmament and the UN Disarmament Commission. The United Kingdom permanent delegation to the 18-nation Geneva conference moved en masse to New York in 1965 when, for the first time in many years, the full Disarmament Commission was convened. In addition to this permanent delegation, officials from the department, or from the Legal Adviser's staff, may be sent out as necessary while the Ministry of Defence also attaches an officer to the delegation when the Conference is in session in Geneva. The military adviser on the United Kingdom permanent mission in New York has not been at all involved in the work of the Disarmament Commission: his tasks have related to short-run peacekeeping and enforcement actions. Informal consultations take place with the three NATO members on the Geneva Conference (United States, Canada and Italy), before any United Kingdom proposal is tackled at either the Geneva Conference or in the UN Disarmament Commission, while the Commonwealth nations involved (India and Nigeria) are also kept closely in touch with developments.

The Arms Control and Research Unit. This small Unit serving both the head of the delegation to the Geneva Conference and the Minister of State for Disarmament, has been engaged on writing policy and research papers, but it is not engaged in administration. There exists a Foreign Office Research Department, which had a disarmament section before the Unit was started, but the department was engaged largely upon historical and factual research. Some of the staff of the Unit have been loaned from the Research Department, others from the Atomic Energy Disarmament Department and the Ministry of Defence, while yet others have been newly recruited from academic life. The Unit is free from the obligations of policy administration. It prepares no ministerial speeches and provides no answers to parliamentary questions. Close relationships are maintained with the Planning Department described further on, and of course, with the Ministry of Defence. The Foreign Office is the only ministry to *initiate* disarmament, but it is the Ministry of Defence which pronounces on all military aspects of disarmament, and thus effectively holds a veto. Moreover, the Deputy Secretary of State for Defence and Minister of Defence for the Army has disarmament as one of his responsibilities. Curiously enough, there has been no specific disarmament section within the Ministry of Defence, although a distinguished scientific adviser, Sir Solly Zuckerman, has advised the Ministry of Defence on disarmament and has gone straight to the Foreign Secretary, not necessarily through the Minister for Disarmament, on any disarmament matter.

No one in the Arms Control and Research Unit appears to have a specialist knowledge of the UN. The day to day tactics at the Geneva Conference are no concern of the Unit, although the director of the Unit stays in close touch with the delegation and sees most of the telegrams. In the preparation of its work, the Unit usually consults the appropriate Foreign Office and Commonwealth Relations Office departments at the drafting stage, and its paper then goes to the Ministry of Defence for comment. Although it has taken over some of the work of the long-term planners in the area of disarmament, the Planning

Department is still nearer the centre of power and has not forfeited all its interest in disarmament.

The Planning Department. Since 1957 a formal Planning Section has existed in the Foreign Office and another planning unit was started in 1959 in the Commonwealth Relations Office. Until 1963 the Foreign Office Planning Section consisted of a Counsellor, a First Secretary, and one other person; while the Commonwealth Relations Office planning staff consisted of four officers who combined policy planning with the writing of research papers. The Plowden Report of the Committee on Representational Services Overseas[4] in 1964 devoted considerable attention to the function of the planners, and made certain specific recommendations which have since been carried out. The separate planning sections were abolished and, as the Report urged, the planning staff was relieved of their coordinate functions, such as organizing briefs for ministerial visits and speeches.

The report states admirably the proper functions of the planner, and the difficulties inherent in his task:

> First, there has to be a mechanism by which to select the most important from the many possible subjects for policy planning studies. Second, a means has to be found of providing staff who are free enough from current work to be able to germinate and develop ideas without being so remote from current work that their thinking becomes too academic. Third, policy planning papers must be studied and taken into account by senior officers with the firm responsibility for taking effective further action. Fourth, there has to be interdepartmental machinery to coordinate studies in the field of foreign policy with defense policy and financial policy. Finally, there must be a means of bringing these studies and recommendations on them to Ministers.[5]

The staff now concentrates on issues that are likely to arise in the next two to five years and attempts to avoid papers that are simply generalized statements of British policy, usually preparing papers that contain specific recommendations addressed to particular problems.

The present three planners maintain a world wide interest, but inevitably tend to specialize in individual topics. One of the Planners is particularly concerned with planning British policy for the UN, including peace-keeping. The planners are sometimes asked to prepare papers by the heads of departments, including the Foreign Office UN departments, and sometimes they will produce papers on their own initiatives.

---

[4]The Plowden Committee met in 1962-63, having been appointed by the Prime Minister. Its report was published in 1964, Command Paper No. 2276, pp. 55-58.

[5]*Ibid.*, par. 218, p. 55.

They are entitled to attend all of the Foreign Secretary's meetings with the Foreign Office and thus they will have the Minister's ear as well as the necessary papers.

A paper written by the planner most intimately concerned with UN policy, for example, would usually be done after consultation with the heads of the departments concerned, especially the Foreign Office UN departments, then put before the Planning Committee consisting of the Under Secretary in charge; other members of the Planning Staff; the Librarian, who, as head of the Research Department, provides the necessary factual information; the head of the political Under Secretary's Department, who provides liaison with the military; and anyone else who has a particular interest in the subject under discussion. The paper might then proceed to a Steering Committee, which meets *ad hoc* and is presided over by a Permanent Under Secretary, then go on to a particular Whitehall committee; or to a Minister if it contains proposals requiring ministerial consideration; or, on occasion to the Cabinet itself. The Foreign Secretary is always informed of the decisions of the Steering Committee. He may accept a proposal outright, or suggest calling a certain committee, or consult his colleagues by asking for a draft minute to individual ministers, or even put the matter to the Cabinet.

The Legal Advisers. The Legal Staff of the Foreign Office comprises the Chief Legal Adviser (known simply, as *the* Legal Adviser), a Deputy Legal Adviser, three counsellors, and seven assistant legal advisers. All of them 'look after' specific departments in the Foreign Office, and thus each Department has its own individual legal adviser to whom it will refer. The more junior legal advisers will usually be assigned to fairly 'non-political' departments, and departments which require sophisticated political judgment as well as legal expertise will be advised by more experienced lawyers. The Legal Adviser himself is responsible for advising the United Nations (Political) Department. He thus advises on the legal aspects of a wide range of UN issues. Other than this, his functions are becoming increasingly supervisory and administrative as the size of his staff increases. The UN (Economic and Social) Department has a different lawyer for advice, and he will show politically important questions to the Legal Adviser while handling all day to day work himself. Legal advisers usually advise a particular department for a three to five year period: as always, the aim is experience and continuity without the sacrifice of flexibility and freshness of approach. Since the Plowden Report, legal advisers for the Commonwealth Relations Office have been recruited by the same machinery as those for the Foreign Office. A candidate appears before a Selection Board convened by the Civil Service Commission, on which

14

the Foreign Office Legal Adviser usually sits or is represented (and usually including an 'outside' professor). The applicant applies through recommendation and interview, but does not sit an examination.

There exists a standing instruction to heads of Foreign Office departments to consult legal advisers at the earliest stage — especially in respect of any draft agreements which are being contemplated. The legal advisers certainly have the right to take the initiative in drawing attention to a particular legal point, but normally they act upon the request of the department concerned or the under secretary or the minister. The function of the legal advisers is to advise the Secretary of State and the Foreign Office departments on all legal matters,[6] and it is commonly said that the task of the legal advisers is to listen to what the government wants to achieve, and then to indicate the legal way of doing it. In fact, this is a little misleading in that it implies a minimal task in the formulation of policy. So far as the UN is concerned, United Kingdom objectives may only be attained within the legal confines of the Charter, and the opinions of the Legal Adviser may not only affect the presentation of policy but may lead to certain alternatives being discarded in favor of others.

The Foreign Office legal advisers also retain overall responsibility for legal advice on the UN specialized agencies, although most of the home ministries which have an interest in the specialized agencies have their own legal staffs, who handle much of the day to day work. But the Foreign Office legal advisers will still be consulted when questions of membership, voting, constitutional amendments, and so forth come up. The Foreign Office Legal Adviser must maintain close links with other ministries interested in international affairs and his relations with the Commonwealth Relations and Colonial Office are especially close. Questions such as Southern Rhodesia in the United Nations are obviously of joint interest to the Commonwealth Relations Office and the Foreign Office UN department — and of joint interest to the respective legal advisers. Equally the question of territorial application clauses in UN multilateral conventions necessitates close consultation with the Colonial Office. The United Kingdom government has taken the position in the UN[7] that where the dependent territory has

---

[6]For an admirable analysis of the role of the Legal Adviser in the broad conduct of international affairs, see the detailed paper by Clive Perry, in *Legal Adviser and Foreign Affairs*, Oceana, New York, 1964, pp. 101-152. See also the review by Judge Fitzmaurice in 59 *American Journal of International Law* (1965) 72-85.

[7]On the UN, the United Kingdom, and territorial application clauses, see R. Higgins, *The Development of International Law Through the Political Organs of the United Nations*, London, Oxford University Press, 1963, pp. 309-316.

some degree of internal self government, the territory's assent is required and local legislation may have to be passed before the convention signed by the United Kingdom can become binding for that territory. Coordination on conventions with territorial application clauses will thus take place between the Foreign Office and the Colonial Office, and may on occasion be required at ministerial level. It may be necessary to set up a special interdepartmental committee, for certain new problems, but even if the main responsibility falls to another ministry, as in the case of UNCTAD, the legal advisers will be consulted; and, as with the conventions on the Law of the Sea, the chief responsibility may fall to the Foreign Office Legal Adviser.

The Foreign Office lawyers play their part, too, in providing legal advice on the instructions to be sent to the permanent mission at the UN. In addition, the mission has on its staff a legal adviser, who is a career legal adviser from the Foreign Office and possibly the United Kingdom today is the only remaining mission with an officer appointed as a legal adviser. The post normally is allocated in order of seniority within the legal staff of the Foreign Office on a three to four year posting. Once on the mission, the legal adviser is responsible to the head of the mission. On some matters he will be in touch directly with the Legal Adviser in London, and on other matters communication will be carried out via the mission channels. Should there be any dispute between the Foreign Office Legal Adviser and the mission's legal adviser, the view of the Foreign Office will prevail. The mission's legal adviser sits on the General Assembly Sixth Committee and helps with all legal matters which arise in the other committees of the Assembly or in other UN organs. Where the UN sets up special committees with significant legal aspects, the Foreign Office may relieve the mission's legal adviser by providing another person to assist in the committee. If any of the UN specialized agencies are holding meetings at which constitutional amendments are likely to be discussed, the Foreign Office will frequently attach a legal adviser to the delegation.

Legal services also exist in other departments that relate to United Kingdom policy in the UN. Not every government department has its own legal advisers (sometimes known as solicitors) though if they do not, they will use the services of the Treasury Solicitor. In addition to the Foreign Office, the Commonwealth Relations Office, the Colonial Office, the Ministry of Education and the Ministry of Overseas Development all have their own legal advisers. The Legal Adviser of the new Ministry of Overseas Development (who came from the Colonial Office) acts as a focal point for liaison with the legal staff of the Foreign Office, Colonial Office, and Commonwealth

Relations Office. In addition, standing counsel are retained by many other ministries. The Ministry of Labour solicitors deal, even insofar as international conventions are concerned, with most of their own international work. This is an exceptional situation, for the treaty making power which lies with the executive is normally conducted through the Foreign Office, but the Ministry of Labour practice arises from the fact that international labour conventions, through treaties, are very similar in content to labour legislation. The Commonwealth Relations Office has a legal staff with special responsibility for the drafting of inter-Commonwealth agreements, but the staff also participates along with the Foreign Office lawyers, in UN conferences of interest to their own Ministry.[8] The legal advisers in the Colonial Office, as well as having an interest in territorial applications clauses, as mentioned above, are concerned also with legal aspects of UN technical assistance and all matters concerning non-self-governing territories. The Home Office has an important Legal Adviser's branch and when domestic legislation has been passed to carry out the terms of treaties whose subject matter falls within the Home Office's province, that office sees to the implementation of the legislation. Moreover, the UN itself takes an interest in many subjects that are the domestic responsibility of the Home Office, such as narcotics and human rights.

The Foreign Office Legal Adviser also has connections with the Law Officers of the Crown. The Law Officers are not usually members of the Cabinet and though the Attorney General has been so on occasion in the past, neither the present Solicitor General nor the present Attorney General is a member of the Cabinet. However, the Attorney General is frequently invited to attend Cabinet meetings. The Law Officers are not necessarily experts in international law, though one or two in recent years have had a considerable knowledge of the subject, and some of them have attended such UN gatherings as the conferences on the Law of the Sea.

It is standard practice for the Foreign Office Legal Adviser to consult the Law Officers before any step is taken on going before the International Court of Justice to settle a dispute. Any decision that might involve the United Kingdom actually appearing before the Court in litigation is thus taken jointly and the same basic practice is believed to exist for advisory opinions of the Court where the United Kingdom might wish to present an oral case or submit written comments. The Attorney General will usually, together with the Foreign Office Legal Adviser, represent the Government in litigation before the Court.

---

[8]See Parry, *op. cit.*, p. 136.

The United Kingdom Permanent Mission at the United Nations

The work of the permanent mission at the UN in New York falls under five main headings: Colonial and Trusteeship, Political, Economic and Social, Financial and Budgetary, and Legal. The two Foreign Office UN departments are responsible for coordinating all instructions and briefs in London while the work of the mission is coordinated internally by the head of Chancery. The Foreign Office will deal primarily with the head of Chancery, sending telegrams and instructions to him unless it is very clear that a particular individual is looking after a particular job.

In London, the procedure is always to clear policy laterally before sending it up the chain of command and before sending out instructions to New York. First, a department view will be formed, then discussed with other departments in the Foreign Office; next a Foreign Office view will be formed, and, if necessary, modified as a result of consultation with other ministries;[9] then a Government view will be formed, after which the mission can be instructed. This procedure does not, of course, have to be followed on every single occasion: once the lines of general policy have been decided, for example, on peacekeeping, the UN (Political) Department of the Foreign Office then deals directly and simply with the mission.

Generally tactics are left to the discretion of the mission. There is a strong belief in the United Kingdom government that the man on the spot is best equipped to make decisions on the timing of a resolution, its co-sponsors, and such tactical matters, though the contents of a proposed resolution will always be cleared with London, and the New York mission will generally be given discretion to agree to variations in its wording after consultation with other missions.

The permanent mission at the UN operates all year, though a London-mounted delegation is sent out for the sessions of the General Assembly. The ECOSOC delegation has been drawn from members of the permanent mission as well as additional London-based delegates and advisers. The United Kingdom is represented on the Trusteeship Council entirely by members of the mission, while the head of the mission or his deputy always represents the United Kingdom on the Security Council and it is extremely rare for the Foreign Secretary to do so.

The Secretary of State for Foreign Affairs has usually led the delegation for the opening debate of the General Assembly and, in-

---

[9]For example, the Colonial Office is consulted on colonial matters; the Commonwealth Relations Office on any Commonwealth question, such as Rhodesia; and the Treasury on financial and budgetary matters.

18

deed, the Prime Minister himself may go. Harold Macmillan led the delegation during his visit to the United States in 1960 and Harold Wilson addressed the 20th General Assembly in 1965. When the Permanent Representative of the United Kingdom to the UN was a member of the Foreign Service, the Assembly delegation was usually headed by a Minister of State from the Foreign Office who stayed for most of the Assembly. It is also usual for two or three parliamentary officials to be members of the delegation for the General Assembly. There has never been any question in British practice, however, of a bipartisan delegation: it has always been a mixture of Government and official designates, without any representation for the opposition political party.

The delegation is supported down the ranks during the General Assembly by extra officials in the form of special advisers, some of whom may be regional specialists, for example, on Latin America, and some of whom may be functional specialists, for example, on disarmament. These special advisers will not necessarily all come from the London Foreign Office — they may come from other posts abroad, such as the Washington Embassy, or from other ministries in London. The delegation is also strengthened by advisers, who help to man the seven main committees of the General Assembly and act as reporting officers. The delegation meets regularly to report upon and discuss the events of the previous day, to look at the day's business in the UN Journal, and to run through the lines to be taken. The head of Chancery will be administratively responsible for this, though the meeting is actually taken by the head of the mission. There have been two information officers in New York, who deal both with the UN press correspondents and with the British information services in New York, and who are concerned with releasing timely statements to match the delegation's tactics in a particular committee and keyed to publishing deadlines of the British newspapers.

Liaison with other missions and delegations to the General Assembly is an important activity, especially as many consultations take place outside formal meetings of the General Assembly and its committees. The regional special adviser will be especially well placed for getting to know the voting intentions and plans of certain groups of countries. So far as lobbying is concerned, it is usually directed at getting support on a particular vote, though of course a continuous attempt is made to persuade on overall policy. The United Kingdom is active in both the Western European caucus and the Commonwealth group, where consultation and lobbying takes place. With two of the seats of the Security Council now being assigned to "Western Europe and others," and five to Afro-Asian countries (and no specific Commonwealth allocation), there has evolved, primarily for election purposes, a new "Western and others" group, including Australia and New Zealand, in which the United Kingdom participates. Normally the caucuses or groups are attended either by the head of the delegation or by the representative who sits on the committee dealing with the subject under discussion.

Continuing relations with the Secretariat are carried out by the permanent mission, with the Permanent Representative dealing with the Secretary-General while the heads of the various sections of the mission seek to establish and maintain close links with their functional counterparts in the secretariat. The usual appointment to the UN mission is for three or four years: it is felt that one or two sessions of the Assembly are necessary to get to know the ropes, but that beyond a four year period there is a risk of staleness.

The small five-man permanent mission to the UN in Geneva is concerned mainly with economic and social questions. The head of the mission is the United Kingdom Representative to the European Office of the UN. He maintains the same close contacts with the Director, European Office of the UN as does the Permanent Representative in New York with the Secretary-General. This mission deals with the several UN meetings held in Geneva; it provides, for example, assistance for the ECOSOC meetings, and helps at the semi-annual meetings of the Executive Committee of the High Commissioner for Refugees. In addition there are a variety of activities of the specialized agencies which require the attention of the Geneva Mission, such as the WHO Assembly, the ILO meetings, the frequent conferences of ITU, and the disarmament conferences. At all these sessions the mission provides political guidance to the British delegation, though the actual briefs will have been prepared in London, and performs representational work at the conferences. Finally, the mission must maintain throughout the year general liaison with other branches of the UN Secretariat which are in Geneva, such as the narcotics section, as well as the secretariats of the specialized agencies.

The Commonwealth Relations Office

Britain's special position in the Commonwealth has required a separate Commonwealth Relations Office. Before Lord Plowden's Committee met to study the Representational Services Overseas,[10] the Commonwealth Service was part of the Home Civil Service, yet it carried out, in effect, a set of international relations separate from those being conducted by the Foreign Office. The Plowden Committee reported adversely on these arrangements, pointing out that a career

---

[10]Plowden Report, *op. cit.*

spent in the Commonwealth Service was, by any yard-stick, a career of overseas service and that the division of the world for representational purposes into Commonwealth and non-Commonwealth countries impeded the development and execution of a coherent foreign policy.

In addition, the Plowden Report made some comments which were directly relevant to the effects of the system existing in 1963 upon UN policy:

> We need a system which recognizes that individual Commonwealth countries have developed regional interests and relationships of their own and cannot regard their relationships with Britain as paramount. The breadth of our representational requirements with Commonwealth countries is perhaps best demonstrated at the United Nations; there members of the Commonwealth express views on every sort of international issue, well beyond the range of Commonwealth affairs. Most of these issues are the primary concern of the Foreign Office and it is the Foreign Office which is responsible for our Mission to the United Nations.[11]

The Plowden Committee felt that the logic of events pointed towards an amalgamation of the Commonwealth Relations Office and the Foreign Office, and that this should be the ultimate objective, but it drew back from recommending that immediate step for fear that it could be misinterpreted as implying a loss of interest in the Commonwealth partnership. What was recommended and later implemented was the creation of a Unified Service to comprise the personnel duties and posts of the Foreign Service, the Commonwealth Service, and the Trade Commission Service, with one combined administration.

At the time of the Plowden Report, the Commonwealth Relations Office had a UN and General Africa Department, but presently the department whose functions bear most directly on the UN is the UN, Western, and Middle East Department. The work of this department includes NATO, East-West relations, the Council of Europe, Antarctica, Aden and the Middle East, and the UN with the specialized agencies. The head of the UN, Western, and Middle East Department is responsible to an Assistant Under Secretary of State who supervises this and two other departments.

Other departments in the Commonwealth Relations Office also have a UN interest. One may point to the Commercial Policy Department which looks after Commonwealth aspects of FAO and UNCTAD, among other subjects. The Cultural Relations Department maintains an interest in Commonwealth aspects of UNESCO; and the Constitutional and Protocol Department, pursuant to Article 102 of the

---

[11]*Ibid.*, par. 42, p. 12.

Charter, includes in its work the registration of British Commonwealth treaties with the UN. Responsibility for Commonwealth policy in the context of the Economic Commission for Africa lies with the Development and Financial Policy and the West Africa departments.

It hardly needs emphasis that there is continuous and close liaison between the Foreign Office and the Commonwealth Relations Office on all UN matters concerning Commonwealth countries. In certain questions the Commonwealth Relations Office will give the policy lead and the Foreign Office will carry out its UN political duties accordingly. Thus, British-Southern Rhodesian relations fell within the general policy lead of the Commonwealth Relations Office, but the Foreign Office played a strong part in handling the Rhodesian problem at the UN, after consultations in the Foreign Office's West and Central Africa Department, and its UN departments. On such major issues, of course, broad guidelines of policy are generally establishd at Cabinet level.

With regard to UNCTAD, the Commonwealth Relations Office maintains close relations with the Board of Trade. A few years ago, it was unusual for Commonwealth Service Officers to do economic or commercial work. In Commonwealth countries that work was done largely by officers of the Trade Commission Service drawn from the Board of Trade, and in foreign countries by Foreign Service Officers. Since the Plowden Report, the Trade Commission Service has been amalgamated in the Unified Service, all of whom undertake economic and commercial duties in both commonwealth and foreign countries, although they are supplemented by officers from the Board of Trade. Some Board of Trade officers have joined the new service, while others have been seconded to it on temporary appointments. Finally, the Commonwealth Relations Office maintains close links with the Ministry of Overseas Development inasmuch as UN technical assistance in Commonwealth countries provides an immediate common interest requiring constant consultation and the Commonwealth Relations Office has been involved in lobbying in Commonwealth capitals on particular issues that include a UN activity.

The Colonial Office

Chapters XI and XII of the United Nations Charter are concerned with non-self-governing and trusteeship territories and these matters, within the British government, fall under the authority of the Colonial Office.

The Secretary of State for the Colonies has two junior ministers (termed parliamentary secretaries), one of whom in 1965 happened to be in the House of Lords while the other was sitting in the House of Commons. The senior civil servants are the permanent Under Secretary and the Deputy Under Secretary of State. Under these senior officials there are six assistant secretaries also responsible to the minister and each of them is in charge of one or more departments in the Colonial Office. Like the Foreign Office, the Colonial Office is divided into geographical departments and subject departments. Falling into the latter group is the International Relations and General Department, whose duties include the UN and colonial matters.[12]

In many ways the responsibilities of this department are more clearly defined with respect to the UN than its counterpart in the Commonwealth Relations Office, for Chapters XI and XII provide the framework of a relationship between the United Kingdom and the UN on colonial questions. There have been over the years a series of questions on non-self-governing territories which have necessitated the evolution of a United Kingdom policy: the scope of Article 73 is among the most obvious, particularly whether or not the Assembly could pass resolutions on the information received under Article 73, and whether such information should include political, as well as economic and social matters.[13] These questions required recommendations by Colonial Office secretaries and approval by ministers. The British attitude to a right of petition from non-Trusteeship territories and the question of visits by the General Assembly Committee of 24 have also required this sort of policy-formulation. Once ministers have settled the broad lines of policy, then the task of the Colonial Office civil servants is clarified in dealing with the continuing stream of items falling within these categories. When a new Government comes to power these established policy guidelines are, of course, open to revision — but they are much more likely to be reconsidered *ad hoc*, when they come up in practice, then *en masse* as part of general policy.

Although the International Relations and General Department is most directly concerned with UN matters, the Social Services Department looks out for colonial matters arising in the context of ILO and since the establishment of the Ministry of Overseas Development, the colonial aspects of FAO and UNESCO have been treated by that ministry rather than the Colonial Office. The Financial Depart-

---

[12]At one stage pressure of work caused the International Relations Department to be divided into two — the practical side, dealing with the General Assembly; and the economic side. They have since been reunified. See Beloff, *op. cit.*

[13]On the history of UN and United Kingdom practice on these questions, see Higgins, *op. cit.*, pp. 113-116.

ment of the Colonial Office, nevertheless, retains an interest in the Economic Commission for Africa, where dependent territories may have associate membership, and in both EPTA and Special Fund questions, coordinating its work on these matters with the Ministry of Overseas Development.

Within the Colonial Office, the head of the International Relations and General Department is constantly in touch with his under secretary, while the under secretary will meet frequently with the parliamentary secretary and the minister. Regular meetings also occur, about twice weekly, between the junior minister and the head of the department. In addition, there are *ad hoc* meetings to which civil servants within the International Relations and General Department will go when the UN topic for which they have particular responsibility arises for discussion. Foreign Office telegrams pertinent to Colonial Office work, including UN matters, are, of course, seen by the under secretary.

Before each session of the UN General Assembly, the Colonial Office joins with the Foreign Office in preparing general speeches and briefs, including instructions on the line to be taken with regard to the Special Committee of 24, and the identification of issues which ought to be referred to ministers or even the Cabinet for policy decisions. Some use is made, for general information purposes, of the International Organization Interdepartmental Committee and major issues will go to the appropriate Cabinet committee. On most UN matters the Colonial Office will go directly to the Foreign Office UN departments. However, if the UN aspect of the issue is, at a particular period of time, comparatively quiescent, then the Colonial Office may go to the head of the appropriate Foreign Office geographical department instead. Questions concerning, for example, Gibraltar or Aden have fallen into this category.

The Colonial Office has also coordinated its work with the Commonwealth Relations Office, for example, with Commonwealth members Sierra Leone, India, Australia, and Tanzania, who sit on the General Assembly Committee of 24, and probably with respect to British protectorates in Southern Africa, a subject of considerable interest to the Commonwealth Relations Office, the Colonial Office, and the Foreign Office. Telegrams on the protectorates, including UN relationships, are circulated among all three ministries, and the United Kingdom Ambassador in Capetown has been kept informed. Within the Colonial Office, the International Relations and General Department handles all UN matters relating to the protectorates, with assistance from the geographical departments.

On the United Kingdom permanent mission to the UN, the head

of one of the five administrative sections, as indicated earlier, handles trusteeship affairs. He has had two people on his immediate staff, one of whom is from the Colonial Office. Although the main responsibility for trusteeship used to lie with the Colonial Office, the United Kingdom in 1965 had only a one-third share in one of the remaining trusteeships, so that the division of responsibility with the Foreign Office was virtually even. In its relations with the permanent mission at New York, the Colonial Office routes telegrams that concern policy through the Foreign Office even if the matter is one of colonial policy. A separate series of telegrams on "domestic matters," such as leaves of absence, travel schedules, and so forth, flow directly between the mission and the Colonial Office. Trans-Atlantic telephone calls between New York and London are quite frequent owing to the urgency of the mission at the UN requiring the consolidated advice of two or more ministries on many issues that arise.

In one sense the work of the Colonial Office has become easier, for, with the gradual emancipation of the British colonies and dependencies, it is a dying service, with a smaller range of issues to cover. On the other hand, those colonies which still remain provide difficult and complex political and economic problems that affect United Kingdom relations with the UN, and fall under the discussions or scrutiny of the international organization.

The Board of Trade

The political minister of this department is known as the President of the Board of Trade. His department plays a significant and interesting role in the conduct of British trade policy through the UN. Changes both in the British governmental system, especially the establishment of the Ministry of Overseas Development, and in the UN institutions, especially the establishment of the UNTAD Board, have affected the Board of Trade's contribution to policy-making on the UN. Other than the Treasury, which has authority over a wide range of matters in British government, the Board of Trade is a good example of the important part that a "home" department can play in matters of international organization; indeed, the Board of Trade, with its far-reaching interests in international trade, has always been more than a "home" department.

The Board of Trade's department, Commercial Relations and Exports (Section I), is the one primarily concerned with UN affairs, although other matters fall within its purview. The senior official is the under secretary, and beneath him there is an assistant secretary whose responsibilities include commodities, GATT and the developing countries, UNCTAD, and general liaison with the Foreign Office over

UN questions. There are two principals in Commercial Relations and Exports (Section I), one of whom deals with commodities and general liaison on UN matters, and the other of whom deals with commercial policy towards the less developed countries, including both GATT and UNCTAD.

The Board of Trade, as its name implies, is concerned with trade rather than aid. The newly established Ministry of Overseas Development has acquired its development functions more at the expense of the Foreign Office than the Board of Trade. The line between overseas development and overseas trade, however, is thin with respect to developing countries. The Ministry of Overseas Development now is responsible, rather than the Foreign Office, for contacts with the UN regional economic commissions, and it both coordinates the briefs and heads the delegations to these commissions. The Board of Trade has sometimes been represented on these delegations. It seems likely, however, that the regional commissions will increasingly devote themselves to trade problems and accordingly the Board of Trade may be expected to play a greater part.

Where questions of major political import arise, the Board of Trade, like other ministries, yields to the Foreign Office. The official response, for example, to pressures from African states for the demotion of Britain from full membership on the Economic Commission for Africa to associate status probably required the decision of the Foreign Office. Similarly, although the Board of Trade has an interest in ECOSOC matters, its views are less influential than those of the Foreign Office, for ECOSOC deals with trade only incidentally.

The greatest influence of the Board of Trade in the formulation and conduct of UN policy undoubtedly lies in the field of UNCTAD. The division of responsibility within Whitehall for most UN questions is rather well established, but when something new occurs, responsibility may be determined *de facto* by events. The Board of Trade and UNCTAD is just such an example. When it became apparent that the developing countries were pressing hard for a world conference on trade and development, the Board of Trade began to prepare briefs and especially to work out the implications with regard to GATT. The basic issue of how far GATT could be made to serve the needs of the developing countries obviously bore directly upon thinking about the UNCTAD.

As the idea of a trade and development conference took shape, the United Kingdom government was faced with the problem of interdepartmental coordination. Some six months before UNCTAD actually took place in Geneva, an interdepartmental committee, under Board of Trade chairmanship, was set up. The various interested departments were represented on this committee, but it reflected in its structure the prime interest of the Board of Trade.

The delegation to the first preparatory committee for UNCTAD, in early 1963, was led by Sir Keith Unwin, who was the Foreign Office official in charge of economic and social affairs on the permanent mission to the UN. The Board of Trade was also represented at this meeting which was concerned with procedural preparations for the conference. In May-June 1963 a second meeting of the preparatory committee was held, this time in Geneva and covering matters of substance. The Board of Trade and the Treasury marked out their particular interests at this point. When the cluster of sub-committees came to be set up, not only was the Board of Trade looking after the manufacturers and the commodities sub-committees, but it also was involved with the committee on institutions.[14] To a large degree, this *de facto* lead from the Board of Trade in the question of UNCTAD institutions has remained, though in the closing stages of the Geneva Conference the Foreign Office had the principal interest in the voting and conciliation aspects of the institutional arrangements. The position whereby the Board of Trade, rather than the Foreign Office, dealt with UNCTAD institutions was arrived at in large measure because of the essential integration of UNCTAD with GATT policy. When it was decided by the UN General Assembly that new trade machinery was required, but was also clear that this did not involve the demise of GATT, the Board of Trade hoped that the UN Trade and Development Board would be established as an organ under Article 64 of the Charter, in relation to ECOSOC, rather than as an Assembly subsidiary organ under Article 22. At the same time, the Government had urged that the secretariat should be an integral part of the Department of Economic and Social Affairs of the UN. Coordination on these questions, including the timing of the intervals between the convening of the Board, and the permanent establishment of the Conference, was carried out through a group under Board of Trade chairmanship, which has continued to the present as the coordination link on policy towards UNCTAD.

At the Geneva Conference in 1964, Edward Heath (then President of the Board of Trade) was the ministerial leader of the United Kingdom delegation. Sir Patrick Reilly, of the Foreign Office, was the senior official; and Sidney Golt of the Board of Trade, was the deputy official leader. The delegation also included officers from the Commonwealth Relations Office and Colonial Office. The Ministry of Agriculture, which had a direct interest in commodities, was represented,

---

[14]The Treasury took the committee on finance and invisibles, and the Foreign Office the committee on procedures.

27

as well as the Treasury, the Foreign Office, and the Board of Trade. At the first meeting of the UN Trade and Development Board in 1965, which was largely procedural, the Board of Trade, the Foreign Office, the Treasury and the Ministry of Overseas Development made up the delegation under Sidney Golt indicating the primary responsibility of the Board of Trade in this new area of UN endeavour.

The Ministry of Overseas Development, which only came into existence after the conclusion of UNCTAD, has taken the development aspects of UNTAD from the Foreign Office and most of the aid functions from the Treasury. Future UNTAD meetings will establish more clearly the division of responsibility in the British government for the promotion of trade policy through the United Nations, with the Board of Trade likely to head the delegation and committees dealing with manufacturing, commodities, and shipping, while the Treasury interests itself in financing, international liquidity, and so forth.

Responsibility for the Intergovernmental Maritime Consultative Organization lies in the shipping department of the Board of Trade. This is the only UN specialized agency on British soil and the relationship between the United Kingdom, as host state, and IMCO, has hardly been glamorous. The presence of a UN agency in London is given little publicity and few people outside of government and the shipping industry are aware of its existence.

Before the return of the Labour Government in October 1964, shipping had been dealt with by the Ministry of Transport. When shipping was moved to the Board of Trade, IMCO questions also came along. IMCO is dealt with by two shipping divisions within the Board of Trade — the Marine Division, which is largely concerned with statutory work, including safety standards, surveying, and so forth, and the Policy Division, which is responsible for handling the non-technical subjects for the 'secretariat' functions of coordinating briefs and clearing them with other departments. This division generally keeps an eye on repercussions on other aspects of shipping policy, and provides a link with the Foreign Office.

Both the Marine and Policy Divisions are headed by undersecretaries. Although the reasons for the movement of shipping from the Ministry of Transport to the Board of Trade have never been fully spelled out in public, it was felt that the Ministry of Transport was getting too large and that the international trade aspects of shipping made the Board of Trade a logical home. Against these arguments has to be balanced the fact that the economic links between shipping and domestic transport are extremely strong and that the tasks of the Ministry of Transport are in no way facilitated by the removal of shipping to another ministry.

IMCO itself deals formally with the Foreign Office, through whom all papers come on to the Board of Trade. Working contacts, of course, are maintained directly between IMCO and the Board of Trade. For the biennial IMCO Assembly papers are prepared in the Marine and Policy Divisions, and briefs are sent in draft to the Foreign Office. If a highly political or complex international legal matter is on the agenda, the Foreign Office itself may prepare a brief. Liaison is also maintained with the Treasury: in addition to its usual watchdog functions, the Treasury will also be consulted on such matters as methods of assessing contributions, but the annual assessed contribution and the contribution of the Government to the IMCO head-quarters building are both taken on the Board of Trade vote.

Policy making for IMCO is very self-contained. The shipping department of the Board of Trade has little need for outside consultation beyond that already mentioned, and very few decisions need to be taken at higher than the under secretary level. Day to day coordination with other departments is done at the level of principals.

The United Kingdom delegation to the IMCO Assembly is usually led by the Board of Trade under secretary in charge of the Shipping Policy Division, with support from the Marine Safety Division and a representative from the Foreign Office. The under secretary heading the Marine Division may also attend for important items. The IMCO Council is normally attended by the assistant secretary in the Policy Division, with support from the Marine Division and the Foreign Office. Reports go up to the Minister of State in the Board of Trade with copies to the Foreign Office and other interested departments. The work concerning the Maritime Safety Committee falls almost entirely to the Marine Division. The delegation to this committee is led by the under secretary of that division, together with administrative and technical support from his division. As all IMCO meetings normally occur in London, it is both possible and desirable to keep the delegations small and to call in additional people as the need arises. This is, in short, a very self-sufficient branch of United Kingdom policy-making with respect to the UN.

The Ministry of Overseas Development

Immediately after the Labour Party was returned to office in October 1964 a new ministry was established in order to project the importance of overseas aid and development and to coordinate more effectively existing policies in this field.

A former Department of Technical Cooperation had dealt with technical assistance aspects of UN affairs through an International Department, which was also responsible, in the technical assistance field, for Organization for Economic Co-operation Development matters, World Bank matters, relations with other bilateral donors, and Commonwealth affairs, making the department rather unwieldly. When the new Ministry of Overseas Development was established, the minister was given Cabinet rank. The senior civil servant, the permanent secretary, was the former Director General of the Department of Technical Cooperation, while the deputy under secretary was drawn from the number two man in the department. Meanwhile, the head of an Economic Planning Staff was appointed at the same level as the deputy under secretary and the under secretary in charge of an International Division was drawn from the Foreign Office.

The International Division of the Ministry of Overseas Development is divided into three departments. First, there is the International Department, whose duties include the development policy aspects of the IBRD and the IMF; second is the Aid Coordination Department, which is concerned with general policy planning; and third is the UN Department, which has direct responsibility for the Special Fund and Expanded Programme for Technical Assistance, as well as coordinative responsibility for the aid aspects of the specialized agencies.

The prime responsibility for the regional commissions of ECOSOC has now been moved to the Ministry of Overseas Development; in overseas missions the liaison officers to the ECA, ECLA, and ECAFE are now asked to communicate directly with the Overseas Development Ministry, except on purely political matters, which are the province of the Foreign Office. ECE, however, has not been moved to the Ministry of Overseas Development, since it is still regarded as being in large part a forum for political exchange with eastern Europe.

Responsibility for FAO has also been moved to the Ministry of Overseas Development from the Ministry of Agriculture, Fisheries, and Food. Although the National Resources Department of the Ministry of Overseas Development has dealt with development aid aspects of the FAO, when an FAO policy matter is common to the development aid policies and activities of all specialized agencies, the UN Department has responsibility for coordination. Indeed, the UN Department deals with any problems that are common to the specialized agencies or involve the UN generally; often these problems will entail going beyond the Ministry of Overseas Development, for they affect those agencies which still fall under functional ministries, such as WHO in the Ministry of Health, ILO in the Ministry of Labour, and ICAO in the Ministry of Aviation. Liaison, of course, is always maintained with the Foreign Office. The distinction between the responsibilities of the UN Department in the Ministry of Overseas

Development and the UN Economic and Social Department of the Foreign Office in the coordination field is that the former coordinates development aid aspects of the work of the specialized agencies whereas the latter exercises general coordination, although, in fact, the demarcation is fairly blurred.

The work of ECOSOC is so massive in its scope that no attempt has been made to shift it from the Foreign Office — though the Ministry of Overseas Development now takes the prime role in development aspects. The main responsibility for UNCTAD, as explained earlier, lies with the Board of Trade, but UNCTAD questions cut across many ministries and special coordinating efforts have been needed. The International Department of the Ministry of Overseas Development deals with the aid functions of UNCTAD and with the Treasury over the IBRD and the IMF. Although prime responsibility for these institutions still lies with the Treasury, the contributions to IDA, for example, are treated as part of the United Kingdom's aid program.

The relationship between the Ministry of Overseas Development, Colonial Office, and Commonwealth Relations Office is of major importance. By far the greater part of the United Kingdom aid program goes to dependent territories and Commonwealth territories, so that constant consultation between these three ministries is required. Specifically, the dependent territories receive aid from the UN through the Special Fund and EPTA. When a proposal for such aid comes either from the United Kingdom or from the territory itself, the Ministry of Overseas Development will take the initiative. However, the Colonial Office is in every respect a co-equal here, because the Colonial Office has Parliamentary responsibility for the administration of these territories. The Treasury also has an interest, for Special Fund or EPTA projects may attract local costs in a dependent territory, and that dependent territory may be grant-aided. Hence the Treasury's approval is needed.

This pattern of division of responsibility between the Ministry of Overseas Development and other ministries is repeated in the method of communication with the permanent mission to the UN in Geneva and New York. On EPTA and Special Fund matters, the ministry will write direct to New York, sending a copy to the Foreign Office; if broader issues are raised, the Foreign Office will be asked for clearance first. Equally, the Treasury will be asked for clearance on letters which bear on financial matters. So far as telegrams are concerned, the Foreign Office telegram system is used by the Ministry of Overseas Development for matters of major importance, while for telegramming mere detail, the ministry will communicate directly with New York.

The relationship between the Ministry of Overseas Development and the Treasury is interesting, because the British contribution to EPTA and the Special Fund is, of course, not arrived at by obligatory UN scale assessment. These items are specifically allocated in the Estimates, and are taken on the Ministry of Overseas Development vote. The head of the UN Department works out an estimate in cooperation with the ministry's finance experts, with a preliminary case for it put to the Treasury by correspondence, followed by negotiations. The minister is usually not involved in negotiating specific items, but rather the aid allocation as a whole. Like other countries, the United Kingdom also has to meet the problem presented by the fact that the UN pledging conference is held in November before the United Kingdom financial year.

The formulation and administration of United Kingdom policy on UNESCO merits special examination. In October 1964 responsibility for UNESCO was taken from the Ministry of Education and placed in the Overseas Development Ministry. The move was precipitated by a reexamination of government policy towards that agency.

It is a commonplace to observe that the program of UNESCO has now moved far from its original emphasis on intellectual cooperation as the path to peace. The question of development and assistance was in the early years of the organization very much in the background, although the constitution always envisaged the active participation of non-governmental organizations. Governments have the duty to enlist the cooperation of their cultural and scientific bodies, preferably by setting up a national advisory commission. Such a body was set up in the United Kingdom, which gradually spawned committees and subcommittees. As this committee structure for intellectual cooperation grew more and more cumbersome, the emphasis in UNESCO began to change from intellectual cooperation towards aid. As more developing countries joined in UNESCO, this shift in balance became accentuated. The repercussions were felt in Whitehall because a non-governmental committee structure could not really deal with such work. The Commonwealth Relations Office and the Colonial Office both had an interest in the UNESCO aid program, while the Treasury also had interests to protect, particularly since UNESCO was situated in Paris and raised the perennial British balance of payments problem. Indeed, policy largely aimed at keeping down the overall UNESCO budget. The Foreign Office also became involved when Russia began to show some interest in UNESCO in 1956.

In 1958 the coordinating body of the United Kingdom non-governmental organizations, the United Kingdom National Commission, strongly urged government reorganization to meet the changing circumstances of UNESCO. The Minister of Education approved the suggestion that a new and less cumbersome committee of 28 individuals (not representing the non-governmental organizations) should be set up to advise the government both on methods of implementing UNESCO's program in the United Kingdom and on what the government should propose for inclusion in that program. In addition, ten specialist advisory committees were set up.[15] Since three of the committees were in fact joint committees of other bodies, an element of indirect non-governmental participation remained.

In sum, there has been a clear policy determination in favor of greater governmental control over UNESCO policy for the aid and financial reasons indicated above. Although the ten specialist advisory committees were intended to give more weight to the opinion of distinguished individuals, in practice non-governmental organization influence still prevails. But the most interesting development has been new Whitehall procedures in the light of an increasing UNESCO emphasis on aid.

Until October 1964 UNESCO was within the Ministry of Education, a fact not without its problems, even apart from the increasing development function of UNESCO, for the Minister of Education is only responsible for England and Wales: separate departments exist for Scotland and Northern England, and care had to be taken not to limit UNESCO to "England." Moreover, until the last few months of the Conservative Government, the Ministry of Education had responsibility for schools, but not for universities or research. Without entering the arguments for or against the integration of schools and universities into one ministry, the situation plainly had implications so far as UNESCO was concerned. Coordination with the Foreign Office, Treasury, Colonial Office, Commonwealth Relations Office, Board of Trade and Department of Technical Cooperation had also presented problems and it is not unfair to say that for a period of years United Kingdom policy to UNESCO was largely negative, with perhaps only two ministers of Education having indicated much interest in that agency.

Accordingly, UNESCO was assigned to the Ministry of Overseas Development when that new Ministry was established by the Labour Government in October 1964. The UNESCO budget has doubled in

---

[15]They cover the following aspects of UNESCO's work: 1. Arts; 2. Comparative Law; 3. East-West projects; 4. Education; 5. Humanities; 6. Libraries; 7. Mass communication; 8. Museums; 9. Natural Sciences; and 10. Social Sciences.

six years and two-thirds was spent on aid in 1965. As the prime task of the Overseas Development Ministry is to coordinate all United Kingdom aid activities, it was a natural home for UNESCO. It is something of an irony that UNESCO should go to Overseas Development at a time when the Ministry of Education has become the Ministry of Education *and Science,* but on balance, the Overseas Development Ministry would seem the proper agency — not least because it maintains closer links with the Foreign Office and the Treasury than did the former Ministry of Education. UNESCO matters fall functionally under the Overseas Development Ministry Education Department, *not* the International Department, so that structural links with Education have not been entirely cut, while FAO is looked after by the Natural Resources Department, again not the International Department.

It is always dangerous and sometimes foolish for those outside of government machinery to hazard opinions, but it seems that there is a good case for the responsibility for the UN specialized agencies being in those ministries where their center of gravity most naturally falls. The ILO still falls clearly within the Ministry of Labour and has not been transferred to the Overseas Development Ministry. WHO is a marginal case, but the arguments in favor of leaving it with the Ministry of Health have merit. Where a Specialized Agency naturally comes within the orbit of the Ministry of Overseas Development, as UNESCO and FAO do, then there is everything to be said for centralizing responsibility for them within one ministry. It should be perfectly possible for the Overseas Development Ministry to maintain close coordinative relations with the ministries of Agriculture and Education, without UNESCO and FAO responsibilities being under separate Education and Natural Resources departments. In short, there would seem to be a strong case for a specialized agencies division within the International Department of the Overseas Development Ministry.

The biennial General Conference of UNESCO is attended by a United Kingdom delegation which includes officials and non-officials, with the delegation led by a minister. The delegation is serviced by briefs drawn up by the secretariats of the National Commission, after consulting the advisory committees and government departments, and by political briefs from the Foreign Office, and in the delegation itself. There the officials, because of the prestige of the civil service, are likely to carry considerable weight with the minister.

The Ministry of Labour

The Ministry of Labour has primary responsibility for the formulation and presentation of British Government policy in the International Labour Organization. When the Ministry of Overseas Development was established in 1964, there was some doubt as to whether it should take over responsibility for relations with ILO on technical assistance matters; however, it was concluded that technical expertise in this area lay with the Ministry of Labour and that relations with ILO should not be divided between two different ministries.

Within the Ministry of Labour, responsibility for ILO matters is concentrated in the Overseas Department. The department is divided into two branches, one of which concerns itself with ILO and the other with labor aspects of the OECD and the Council of Europe, as well as liaison with labour attachés at United Kingdom missions overseas. The head of the Overseas Department is at the under secretary level. He reports to the deputy secretary. They are the two government delegates to the International Labour Conference.

The government delegation to the Conference also includes a number of advisers drawn from sections of the Ministry of Labour or from other government departments to deal with the technical items on the agenda, who serve on the committees of the Conference that deal with technical items. The United Kingdom government representative on a committee on underground work in mines, for example, would probably be an official from the Ministry of Power. The government delegation also includes the United Kingdom Permanent Representative to the UN office in Geneva. The Minister of Labour usually attends the Conference briefly to make a speech in the plenary session of the Conference on government policy in relation to problems under examination in the Conference.

The government delegation to the Governing Body meetings usually consists of the deputy secretary and the under secretary, though for certain items an assistant secretary and/or a principal will attend instead. The delegation at the Governing Body also keeps in close touch with the United Kingdom Permanent Representative.

It is felt that the selection of delegates to the Conference and, a fortiori to the Governing Body, from the Overseas Department rather than the technical departments of the Ministry, is desirable because it is here that continuing knowledge of the ILO scene lies.

The inclusion of the United Kingdom Permanent Representative in Geneva in the conference delegation and close contact with him during Governing Body sessions serves several useful purposes: first, it provides someone who can either deal with or advise on the political questions that arise, such as a resolution on disarmament; second, the Permanent Mission provides a channel of speedy communication back to the Foreign Office; and, third, the Permanent Mission has a comparative knowledge of events and procedures in the other specialized agencies located at Geneva, which is especially relevant to matters of staffing, salary scales, and so forth.

The tactics and methods of approach by the United Kingdom Government to ILO matters are to a large extent influenced by the unique tripartite system of representation to the organization. A pattern of two government votes to one employer vote and one worker vote obtains in both the Conference and the Governing Body. From the United Kingdom government point of view, the pattern of support required to carry any particular proposal usually consists of "Western" oriented governments, plus at least either the complete employers' group or the complete workers' group.

Draft texts of conventions and recommendations for adoption by the Conference are circulated well in advance while briefs are prepared by the Overseas Department in consultation with the appropriate technical sections of the Ministry of Labour, and, where necessary, with other government departments. For example, the ministries of Power, Transport, and Pensions and National Insurance have frequently contributed to the preparation of Conference briefs, while the Ministry of Technology and the Board of Trade may also contribute to technical advice respecting labor.

Draft resolutions tabled at the Conference usually deal with more general and, in some instances, highly political matters. Normally they must be submitted two weeks before the Conference opens, while briefs for these are also prepared by the Overseas Department after the kind of consultations indicated above. On certain political matters, such as a resolution to expel or suspend a member state from the Organization, there is close consultation with the Foreign Office to ensure that United Kingdom policy in ILO will be consistent with the policy in other bodies.

Technical assistance matters, which are a growing aspect of the Organization's work, are mainly dealt with in the Governing Body. The views of the Ministry of Overseas Development are sought by the Ministry of Labour on all Governing Body papers dealing with technical assistance matters. Since certain extra-budgetary expenditure on technical assistance projects executed by ILO are financed from the United Nations Special Fund and EPTA and since Overseas Development carries on its vote the contributions to those agencies, the Ministry of Overseas Development could make inquiries and complaints to the UNDP Governing Council[16] about the way in which

---

[16]Beginning in 1966 the Special Fund and EPTA had a single Governing Council of thirty-seven members under the new United Nations Development Programme.

money from these agencies was being used by ILO. The United Kingdom contribution to the ILO budget, including provision for technical assistance within the ILO budget, is borne on the Ministry of Labour vote.

In preparing its final briefs for the Conference delegation, the Ministry of Labour, mindful of the difficulties inherent in the ILO voting system, makes a point of not tying the delegation's hands too closely before they go to Geneva, since they will need to concert their line with friendly delegations on the spot. Consultations in Geneva, before the opening of the Conference, take place with Commonwealth and other friendly delegations with a view toward agreeing upon a line of policy. Contacts will also be made with the workers' and employers' representatives, especially those from the United Kingdom. It is felt that it is more profitable for consultations with the United Kingdom worker and employer representatives to take place in Geneva after they have had a chance to align their views with those of their colleagues, rather than in London where they are not yet in a position to commit themselves. As the workers' and employers' groups are much more cohesive than the governments', a knowledge about the line they are proposing to take is of particular importance. The day to day tabling of amendments during committee discussion on draft conventions and recommendations and on resolutions makes rapid decisions essential, though as the committees' reports come before the plenary session in the final stages of the Conference there can be reference back to the Ministry of Labour or to other Whitehall departments if necessary before the final vote.

The three annual sessions of the Governing Body provide the Overseas Department of the Ministry of Labour with a considerable work load. For the Governing Body sessions, papers are prepared in the main by the International Labour Office, but as they are frequently circulated only shortly before the Governing Body session, consultation on them in Whitehall is hasty and too cursory. The same tactical considerations apply as in the Conference.

The Governing Body carries out a detailed examination of the budget. The Director General's proposals are usually circulated well in advance and examined in detail by the Ministry of Labour, which decides the line to be taken by the delegation after consultation with the Treasury and the Foreign Office and before the delegation goes to Geneva. Any supplementary item to the budget which is not circulated until the delegation gets to Geneva has to be dealt with on the spot, though consultation with Whitehall is possible by telegram or telephone. The delegation is usually accompanied at the budget session by a representative of the Ministry of Labour's Finance Department.

Any advice which may be necessary on the legal aspects of the texts of conventions or recommendations can be provided by the ministry's own Legal Department, but preparation of formal instruments of ratification of conventions, which impose treaty obligations on member states, is handled by the Foreign Office legal advisers.

Resolutions adopted by the Conference usually call for action by the Governing Body. This may take the form of requesting the Governing Body to consider the inclusion of particular items on future Conference agendas for the adoption of conventions or recommendations. In such cases, the Overseas Department of the Ministry of Labour carries out any necessary consultations with technical departments of the ministry or with other government departments in preparation for discussion of the action to be taken by the Governing Body. In the case of resolutions dealing with more political matters, the Governing Body may be requested to take action with individual member states. For example, in 1965 a resolution requested the Governing Body to press the government of Portugal to implement the recommendations of an ILO commission of inquiry on the use of forced labor in Portuguese African territories. On such matters, the line to be taken by the delegation to the Governing Body would be prepared in consultation with the Foreign Office.

The Ministry of Aviation

The Ministry of Aviation is involved in British policy making for the UN by virtue of the United Kingdom's membership in the International Civil Aviation Organization. The United Kingdom is a member of both the ICAO Council and the Air Navigation Commission. The former body sits continuously, a fact which permits member governments a fairly substantial control over the activities of the secretariat. The United Kingdom is both an economy-minded nation and a leader in the field of civil aviation.[17] These two factors influence Ministry of Aviation attitudes towards ICAO, for while the government endeavors to play a role in ICAO commensurate with British standing in civil aviation, it also tries to prevent too great an expansion of the ICAO budget and to get — as the ministry puts it — "value for money."

The broad outlines of British policy towards ICAO have been laid down for some years and to some extent the Ministry of Aviation has

---

[17]Thus the International Standards and Recommended Practices, annexed to the ICAO Convention, are regarded by the United Kingdom as merely providing a minimum standard above which British aviation practice has already passed.

38

regarded its task as one of keeping the machine well oiled. Within the ministry, beneath the permanent secretary, there are three deputy secretaries, one of whom has responsibility for matters that include ICAO.

The overall coordination on ICAO within the ministry is done by the Aviation Overseas Policy Division, with a special department for the circulation of all Montreal documents both to and from ICAO and within Whitehall itself. The particular work relating to ICAO is divided functionally within the ministry. Particular agenda items may go to the Flight Safety Directorate, or Air Traffic Control, or other departments. The Foreign Office is consulted on political matters, the Treasury on establishment questions, and the Commonwealth Relations Office, the Colonial Office, the Ministry of Defence, the Overseas Development Ministry, and the Post Office as circumstances dictate. Technical briefs are generally sent out directly to the ministry concerned while the broader issues are circulated through the International Organizations Committee.

The delegation to the ICAO Assembly is headed by the deputy secretary, who attends the first seven to ten days, largely to keep an eye on the ICAO elections. The delegation is then left in the charge of the ICAO Council member, who is an assistant secretary. A ministry of Aviation legal adviser sits on the legal commission; and a statistician-economist sits on the economic committee. The Ministry of Aviation also provides delegates to the administrative committee and the technical committee. It is unusual for the Foreign Office to be directly represented, but if a major political problem arises, such as South African membership, then a Foreign Office official attached to the United Kingdom Permanent Mission in New York may be called upon if the meeting is in Montreal. Where the meeting is a regional one, such as the ICAO regional meeting in Rome, then the head of the mission will look to the local British Embassy for political guidance.

The Ministry of Aviation holds frequent consultations with the major airlines, including, of course, the large nationalized firms of BOAC and BEA. In the program initiated by ICAO to provide international cost sharing for ground aids, such as weather ships servicing the North Atlantic route, the territorial countries, Greenland (Denmark) and Iceland, could not be expected to bear the costs. ICAO devised a scheme whereby the countries whose airlines used this route were charged for the purchase and maintenance of the navigation aids. The United Kingdom contributes some £375,000 per annum to this programme and, in principle, the government expects reimbursement from the airlines. But the government has indicated that reimbursement must be within the context of the economics of airline operation and since civil aviation is still a subsidized industry, no levies have been made upon the airlines.

The United Kingdom pays approximately ten percent of the total ICAO budget, amounting to a contribution of some £175,000-£200,000 per annum. However, four-fifths of the budget is determined by ICAO's participation in the UN technical assistance activities financed by the Special Fund and EPTA. The finance committee of the ICAO Council prepares estimates for three years, which are referred to the Treasury. Parliamentary estimates, of course, are presented by the Treasury on a yearly basis, so that in effect the Treasury commits Parliament for three-year support of ICAO. So far as technical assistance is concerned, the Ministry of Overseas Development has acquired an interest in ICAO because of the ministry's interest in EPTA and the Special Fund, but the Ministry of Aviation still provides the personnel and training establishments under technical assistance programs.

Ministry of Health

United Kingdom policy in the World Health Organization falls within the authority of the Ministry of Health. The International and Food Division scrutinizes the WHO agenda and allocates the technical items for the preparation of briefs. The Foreign Office looks after the political aspects and, like the Ministry of Health, coordinates the views of other interests which it may consult. The final briefings are circulated through the International Organization Committee, though they are not usually formally considered through that committee. While WHO meetings are actually in progress, cables are being sent continuously to Whitehall through the Foreign Office and a final report is presented to the International Organization Committee.

The delegation to the WHO consists of government officials, though there have been pressures for the inclusion of representatives of certain non-governmental organizations, such as the British Medical Association. The Ministry of Health, however, has insisted that these bodies should not take part in British policy making at the delegation level. The delegation is headed by the Chief Medical Officer of the Ministry of Health while Scotland's interests are maintained by the presence of the Chief Medical Officer for Scotland. The Chief Medical Adviser of the Ministry of Overseas Development is also included as well as the head of the International Department who provides administrative expertise. The permanent United Kingdom mission in Geneva provides political advisers to the delegation.

The United Kingdom has been budget conscious with WHO as well as with other UN specialized agencies, and the government has never contributed to the joint voluntary funds established, mainly by Scandinavian initiatives, for malaria, smallpox, and water programs. United Kingdom delegations have urged the merits of collective financial responsibility as against voluntary contributions, but when growing funds for malaria eradication were returned in large part to the regular budget, the British government, having urged collective financial responsibility, found itself paying its assessed share of an enlarged budget, a practice hardly nearer to the Treasury's heart than voluntary contributions. From the Treasury's point of view the worst of both worlds may have been achieved. Voluntary funds still exist while the main costs for activities started under them have been shifted to the regular budget.

The present position with regard to WHO is not an entirely happy one. The Foreign Office, in its laudable attempts to coordinate policy on the specialized agencies, may be attempting to impose common techniques and standards that are impossible to attain. At the same time, in spite of high level decision to the contrary, some feeling may remain that the WHO work of the Ministry of Health should be transferred to the Overseas Development Ministry: The really difficult case is the technical assistance aspects of WHO's work, which now takes up half of the WHO budget. The Ministry of Overseas Development has argued that any expansion of technical assistance work should properly be financed from the UN Special Fund and EPTA,[18] and the UN contribution to these funds has been taken on the Overseas Development Ministry's vote. On the other hand, the WHO Assembly would strenuously argue against splitting off WHO technical assistance from the regular budget and the mainstream of WHO policy-making. WHO is unique among the specialized agencies of the UN, for the technical assistance function is written into its constitution and the Minister of Health can make a strong case against a division of responsibilities.

The Post Office

The Post Office is one of the most self contained of all government departments by the highly technical nature of its work and it is the ministry responsible for the two technical specialized agencies, the International Telecommunication Union and the Universal Postal Union. The political minister of the Post Office is the Postmaster General. The senior official, the permanent secretary, is the Director General. Immediately below him are three deputy directors general, one of whom has general responsibility for ITU and UPU. These

---

[18]As, for example, in the case of ICAO.

senior civil servants form the general directorate of the Post Office concerned with broad policy questions. Beneath the general directorate there are eleven departments headed by directors at the under secretary level. One of these, the Radio Services Department, divides into two branches one of which, the Radio Branch, plays the major role in the formulation and presentation of United Kingdom policy in ITU. ITU has been placed in the Radio Branch rather than the External Telecommunications Executive, largely because ITU is regulatory in character while the External Telecommunications Executive is geared to operational matters, but the latter department does participate in the International Telegraph and Telephone Consultative Committee as laid down in Article 5 (d) of the ITU Convention.

The British administration also has to prepare for the intermittent plenipotentiary conferences, administrative conferences, and the Administrative Council meetings of ITU. The Post Office formulates, in consultation with other ministries, United Kingdom policy on the possible revision of the convention governing ITU, its future work, policies, membership, and expenditure, all of these matters falling within the purview of the Plenipotentiary Conference.

The United Kingdom is a member of the Administrative Council, which consists of the representatives of twenty-nine countries and acts on behalf of the Plenipotentiary Conference as the governing body of the ITU. As the Administrative Council meets for four to five weeks each year, with about fifty agenda items, it is around this Council that the bulk of administrative ITU work in the Post Office revolves. The Radio Branch of the Radio Services Department has broad discretion in its briefs for the Administrative Council and no formal clearance of these briefs through the International Organization Committee is required. Even political and membership matters concerning ITU are assigned within the Radio Branch, although the General Department of the Foreign Office will be consulted on any special issues that arise. The Director of the Radio Services Department or the head of the Radio Branch attend the Administrative Council each year.

The United Kingdom representative to the Administrative Council is in principle not there to put the United Kingdom view, for Council members are selected by the Plenipotentiary Conference to promote the objectives of ITU, and his assistant is chosen from the Radio Branch. At the Plenipotentiary Conference of 1965, however, the delegation also included two Foreign Office officials, one of whom was concerned with political issues and the other of whom was a legal adviser on ITU matters. The Radio Branch of the Radio Services Department prepared reports upon return from both the Administrative Council and Plenipotentiary Conference which were circulated to all interested ministries through the International Organization Committee. Any international conventions resulting from the work of ITU will be published as a Command Paper and laid before the House of Commons for ratification in the normal way.

The Post Office, through its Engineering Department and External Telecommunications Executive takes an active part in all aspects of the technical work of the ITU and through consultative committees it coordinates its preparation for this work with other government departments and industry as necessary. The procedures followed by the Post Office with respect to the Universal Postal Union are not dissimilar.

UPU is the responsibility of the Overseas Mails Branch, which is one of five branches in the Postal Services Department. The Overseas Mails Branch is itself divided into four divisions, one of which deals specifically with UPU constitutional and political questions, and customs matters while another is concerned with the more technical aspects of the UPU convention and agreements. The greater part of the preparatory work is done in these two divisions for the UPU Congress which meets every five years. If United Kingdom proposals affecting constitutional matters of UPU are being considered, the Foreign Office will be consulted. Other ministries will be involved as appropriate. For example, discussions will be held with the Ministry of Aviation on certain aspects of airmail conveyance charges that might affect the airline companies or the Board of Trade with respect to shipping mail freights, and so forth. Each ministry is asked by the Post Office to comment on relevant proposals and offer suggestions. The same practice is followed with regard to propositions that other countries put forward to the UPU Congress. At any one Congress, some 1500-2000 proposals may be put forward and the United Kingdom delegation needs to be briefed on all of them. In addition to the Post Office briefs, the Foreign Office, the Commonwealth Relations Office, and the Colonial Office provide political briefings. The Colonial Office interest lies in the separate representation in UPU and ITU (one seat) for the "British ensemble" of still dependent territories.

At the UPU Congress most proposals are first discussed in committee and committee decisions must be ratified by the Congress in its plenary session. However, as most of the committees consist of all the members of the Congress, points are not usually raised anew in plenary unless special reasons exist for thinking that a committee decision can be reversed. At the Congress the leader of the United Kingdom delegation is a senior Post Office official and the Foreign Office is represented either by officials from London or the local

British Embassy. Other departments are not represented. Decisions of the Congress, where appropriate, are incorporated into regulations made under the United Kingdom Post Office Act, using the statutory instrument procedure, while constitutional provisions need to be published as a Command Paper and ratified. As with the procedure for ITU, a report is made upon the results of Congress through the International Organization Committee to interested ministries.

Considerable preparation is also required for the annual meeting of the UPU Executive Council. The United Kingdom is a member of the Council which is responsible for running the organization between congresses. The United Kingdom also attends a yearly management meeting of the Consultative Committee on Postal Studies. These two bodies provide the bulk of day to day UPU work for the Overseas Mails Branch of the Post Office.

The high degree of autonomy in the Post Office is reinforced in the area of international organization by the fact that the Post Office budget does not come from voted monies, with the exception of the ministers' salaries. The practice here is quite different from all other ministries which have responsibility for UN questions. The United Kingdom contributions to both ITU and UPU come from the Post Office's own budget and since this is not controlled by a vote on the Estimates, the Treasury is not involved.

The Home Office

The Home Office is the department primarily responsible for advising the Government on matters within the scope of the UN Narcotics Commission. The United Kingdom representative to the Commission is a Home Office official. This aspect of Home Office work stems from the ratification of the Opium Convention of 1912 which was contained in the Treaty of Versailles. As the Home Office has responsibility for commerce in dangerous articles, it was deemed to be the appropriate coordinating ministry.

The Home Office is also responsible for the implementation of any legislation within its sphere of competence that has been passed pursuant to British adherence to an international treaty. With respect to ILO, for example, the Home Office participates in the preparation of questionnaires and has responsibility for the ratification of the conventions as well as consultations with the employers and workers affected by such conventions.[19]

A Home Office official also sometimes represented the United

---

[19]See Donald G. Bishop, *The Administration of British Foreign Relations,* Syracuse University Press, Syracuse, N. Y., 1961, p. 313.

Kingdom on the UN Human Rights Commission, and on the Social Commision of ECOSOC.

The Treasury

The Treasury, headed by the Chancellor of the Exchequer, has both a general and specific role in the formation of British policy in the UN. The general responsibility lies in the Treasury's control over annual departmental expenditure. At the same time, the Treasury is not formally responsible for UN policy, even with regard to budgetary matters, for the Foreign Office answers to Parliament on overall UN budgetary questions. There are specific additional duties upon the Treasury in that it is the Department responsible for IMF and IBRD.

Not only does the Treasury seek to keep down overall expenditure, but it tries, by the distribution of expenditure between departments, to establish a balanced overall pattern. In short, it concerns itself with the ecology of expenditure as well as the level. Moreover, no department can initiate action that requires any new expenditure of funds without Treasury approval. This applies equally to proposed legislation. Thus the Treasury is represented on inter-departmental committees relating to the UN, and attends any meetings involving financial items. When a bill like the International Monetary Fund Bill of July 1965 comes before the House of Commons, the Treasury plays a major role in its formulation. Each ministry with responsibility for any agency in the UN system includes in its estimate the costs of subscriptions, attendance at conferences, participation in voluntary programs, and so forth.

The basic, assessed contribution to the UN for the financial year 1965-66, taken on the Foreign Office vote, was £2,320,000. The estimated assessment for UNEF for this period was a total of £357,170. The British share of expenses of the force in Cyprus was estimated at £357,150[20] and provision was made for repayment to the Ministry of Defence and the Ministry of Public Building and Works for expenses incurred on behalf of contingents other than that from the United Kingdom with the payment of any balance to the UN. The Foreign Office submits in its estimate other items relevant to the UN, such as the salary of the United Kingdom Permanent Representative at the UN, his *frais de répresentation*, and the cost of other home and local staff. The total expenditure for this group of items was estimated at £371,000 compared to £289,000 in 1964-65 and the expenses of United Kingdom delegations going out to UN meetings were estimated at

[20]Originally, non-UN peacekeeping costs in Cyprus were taken on the Commonwealth Relations Office vote, in the Military Assistance section (£1,250,000).

£63,000. The Foreign Office also deals with the Treasury over grants in aid to UNRWA (£1,928,572 for Palestine refugees) and the UN High Commissioner for Refugees (£111,000).

The Overseas Development Ministry negotiates with the Treasury for the voluntary contribution to the EPTA (£1,696,538 in 1965-6) and the Special Fund (£2,500,250). It also took on its vote a grant in aid to UNICEF (£400,000), a contribution of £175 to the Special Fund Locust project, and £1,800 towards an FAO survey on the uses of coconut oil in Chemical Industries. The actual subscription to FAO (10.9% of the total FAO budget) was estimated at £675,500 and to UNESCO (at 6.77% of the budget) at £590,000.

The Treasury is, on the whole, functionalized rather than departmentalized, that is to say, persons are not assigned to the financial and budgetary aspects of particular government departments, but rather to subjects. From the viewpoint of control over UN matters, this has obvious administrative advantages: the estimates concerning UN expenses or projects are watched over by a very small specialist group of people in the Treasury, even though the subject matter spans many ministries. It is not, of course, a question of the Treasury annually being presented unawares with ministry estimates covering UN items; the Treasury is represented at the planning stage of particular projects involving expenditure.

In addition to its general watchdog functions over all expenditure on the UN, the Treasury has direct responsibility for the Bretton Woods agencies. Policy towards IMF is very much in the hands of the Treasury, while the Treasury is now having to learn to include the Overseas Development Ministry in the formation of policy towards IBRD. The British executive directors on the Board of the IBRD and IMF are responsible to the Chancellor of the Exchequer. The Chancellor attends the annual meeting of the Fund and Bank, taking with him such advisers as he needs. These advisers have traditionally come from the Treasury and the Bank of England, and now include representatives of the Ministry of Overseas Development as well.

Staffing, Recruitment, and Training

What sort of men in the United Kingdom government are handling UN affairs? And what training and experience have they for such responsibilities?

UN matters are, of course, handled both by politicians, owing their position to the fact that their party has a majority in the House of Commons, and by career civil servants who remain in office irrespective of party majorities.

At the present moment, those politicians in the United Kingdom having major responsibilities relating to the UN are the Secretary of State for Foreign Affairs, the Secretary of State for Commonwealth Relations, the Minister for Overseas Development and the Secretary of State for the Colonies. The Chancellor of the Exchequer, the Minister of Health, the Minister of Labour, the Minister of Aviation and the Minister of Transport all have responsibilities which bear incidentally upon policy in the UN.

The Secretary of State for Foreign Affairs has normally had considerable experience in foreign affairs, often having held at some stage in his career a Foreign Office portfolio, or at least having been the Opposition front bench spokesman on foreign affairs. He may well have had personal experience of the UN, either as a Minister of State or as one of the parliamentarians who customarily serve brief periods on the delegation in New York. None of this happened to be true of the Secretary of State for Foreign Affairs in 1965, but the exception may prove the rule. Although it is unusual for the Secretary of State not to have had a foreign affairs background he can, with the aid of his civil servants, adapt himself rapidly and successfully to his new field and to an appreciation of the UN as a form of national policy.

The Foreign Secretary has four ministers of state, one of whom is the Permanent Representative to the UN and another of whom has a general responsibility for UN matters. Within the civil service, the chief official, the permanent under secretary, has working directly beneath him the heads of the various departments. In the Foreign Office, the departments are broadly speaking divided into functional, geographical, and economic grouping.[21] As indicated earlier, the Foreign Office's UN departments and the Commonwealth Relations Office's UN, Western, and Middle East departments are the functional departments most directly concerned with UN policy, although the geographical and economic departments bear indirect responsibilities for various aspects of UN work.

The heads of the Foreign Office or the Commonwealth Relations Office UN departments have not necessarily come up through the ranks of their own departments and may have to gain a certain part of their experience while on the job. This would seem to be an example of the British obsession with amateurism in government and unfortunate from the point of view of securing a deep and sympathetic understanding of the UN, but this criticism has largely been removed by recent innovations in "career planning" within the foreign service.

---

[21]Both the Foreign Office and the Commonwealth Relations Office also have administrative, information, and technical departments.

In February 1964 a Committee under the Chairmanship of Lord Plowden reported to the Prime Minister on the representational services overseas and the Report was then presented to Parliament.[22] The Plowden Report observed that certain Foreign Office reforms initiated in 1943 had "undoubtedly [caused] some loss at first in regional, linguistic, and functional expertise." Although later attempts had been made to check this loss, the Committee found it

> fair to conclude that, in the foreign service, the pendulum was allowed to swing too far away from specialization in the post-war years, that the readjustment now taking place is necessary, has some way to go, and should be pressed ahead vigorously. In the Commonwealth Service, the problem of providing specialists, except in information work, has not yet been fully tackled and is urgent.[23]

The attainment of such specialization called for organizational efforts, and the Committee called for "a diligent and unremitting process of career planning."

The Plowden Report also urged, in its most radical recommendation, the unification of the Foreign Service and the Commonwealth Service into a new Diplomatic Service for representation overseas. A unified Diplomatic Service, was, therefore, established although separate Foreign and Comonwealth Relations Offices are still maintained in Whitehall. Considerable emphasis is now given to career planning by the Diplomatic Service Administration Office. Within this office the Personnel Department and various diplomatic service boards[24] will seek to give a man an opportunity to specialize without sacrificing his broad experience. The aim is to provide a man with experience both at home and abroad, largely in political work and diplomacy, with the expectation that within ten years he and his superiors will be able to discover where his particular talents lie for specialization.

At the same time, the benefits of specialization, especially in as complex an area as UN policy and machinery, must be weighed against the continuing need for fresh ideas and approaches. A head of a UN functional department, therefore, is likely to have had some experience of UN matters somewhere along the line, either in a junior position within the department or in conference or mission work abroad. He would ordinarily stay in his post long enough for his

---

[22]Command Paper No. 2276, February 1964.

[23]*Ibid.*, p. 48, para. 188.

[24]Top civil service appointments will be made by consultation at high level. Below that, different diplomatic service boards exist at different levels to advise and recommend on appointments.

department to benefit from his approach and for him to acquire any extra expertise which the complexities of UN work require, but he is unlikely to remain in UN work for the rest of his career.

Every entrant into the Diplomatic Service has the opportunity to make known to the Personnel Department his particular interests, including UN work. All new entrants are required to do a general two-week course, which will usually be followed either by a Treasury Centre Course (covering the structure of government) or a Commercial and Economic Course, arranged by the Board of Trade. Officers taking up a specialist "functional" post for the first time are given a course in the knowledge and techniques they will require. So far as work within the UN departments is concerned, however, the emphasis continues to be on "training on the job." The first assignment of a young civil servant in the field of UN affairs may be as rapporteur at a UN conference and he may later be assigned to the United Kingdom Mission in New York after some service in the UN departments of the Foreign Office, although no established pattern exists. In spite of an emphasis on expertise at the permanent mission, postings for much more than four years are not usually thought desirable, as diplomatic stagnation and over exposure as a lobbyist at the United Nations present a real problem.

Admission to the Foreign Service is gained through recruitment into either the Administrative or Executive grades. Entrants to the Administrative grades are required to hold either a first or second class honours University degree and to pass a short written examination. This is known as Method II. Successful candidates then go before the Civil Service Selection Board, which covers selection for the whole of the civil service, including the home departments. Following the Plowden Report the Foreign Office and the Commonwealth Relations Office have been unified with respect to recruitment and the personnel department of the Diplomatic Services Administration Office now has one representative seated on the Civil Service Selection Board.[25] This stage of the selection process usually involves interviews over about two and one-half days with the screened applicants going on to a board that makes the final selection.

An alternative and equal method for entry into the Administrative grade, entitled Method I, is by means of a long, degree-type examination without the need to go before the Civil Service Selection Board. An ordinary interview is, however, required. For Method I a university degree is not needed. Understandably, candidates who have already taken their university examinations are often reluctant to sit another

---

[25]Previously the Commonwealth Service was regarded as part of the Home Civil Service for purpose of recruitment.

lengthy examination, and hence tend to opt for Method II. Although more people take Method II than Method I each year, the examiners treat both methods equally. In addition, supplementary competitions are held for the Administrative grades of the Foreign Service for candidates between the ages of 25 and 35 who have acquired a particular expertise, but a knowledge of international organizations has not been considered as an attribute that affords preference to a candidate.

A high percentage of the new recruits to the Administrative grades have read classics, or history, or literature at the university. The Oxford degree of politics, philosophy, and economics has been fairly usual among the recruits, but a degree in international relations has been comparatively rare. The reason lies not so much in the traditional English emphasis on the humanities as the necessary background for all subsequent endeavor, but rather in the limited number of universities in the United Kingdom that give degrees in politics or international relations. Neither Oxford nor Cambridge do so and over sixty percent of new Foreign Service entrants still come from these universities. The Plowden Report emphasized that the Civil Service Commission did not deliberately weigh the scales against non-Oxbridge candidates, but it suggested that the Civil Service Commission and the universities should henceforth cooperate in trying to attract and accept candidates from non-Oxbridge universities who met the required standards. This effort is under way. Results will come slowly, but the advantages that Oxford and Cambridge have enjoyed are being challenged not only by other "redbrick" universities but also the newer universities. The Plowden Report is likely to lead toward a greater emphasis on training in such subjects as international relations, especially *within* the Foreign Service, and the integration of the Foreign Office and the Commonwealth Relations Office recruitment allows a larger pool from which to choose specialist knowledge for manning the UN departments.

Much work relating to the UN and the specialized agencies is, of course, done by civil servants in the Home Service, who are recruited like Foreign Service officials, except for compulsory qualifications required for foreign languages. No special training in international work, however, is given to the officials in the technical ministries, leaving the acquisition of experience to the job itself.

Britain and the International Secretariat

The United Kingdom has made significant contributions to a strong and capable international secretariat. Britain had already made her influence felt on this matter in the League of Nations when, with France, she had successfully championed the cause of an international civil service against such countries as Germany and Italy, which had favored the concept of a national secretariat. In 1945, during the drafting of the UN Charter at San Francisco, Britain stressed time and again the need to choose officers on individual merit and not as government representatives; and she has since then steadfastly adhered to the long term wisdom of this view in her policy and practice towards those of her own nationals who serve on the UN Secretariat.

The British government has studiously avoided exerting any influence over her nationals in the UN secretariat. So rigorous has it been in the application of this policy that there have been occasional complaints by United Kingdom nationals in the Secretariat that they were being unfairly ignored by the United Kingdom mission to the UN.[26] This entirely praiseworthy attitude towards the Secretariat has also meant that only very incomplete statistics have been gathered in London on British employees of the UN, as this is regarded as a matter between the individual and the UN. The fairly steady rate of United Kingdom participation in the work of the Secretariat with numbers being considerably higher than the "desirable range" assessed in terms of geographical distribution is shown in Table A.

Table A

UNITED KINGDOM NATIONALS IN UN IN PROFESSIONAL AND
HIGHER LEVEL POSTS SUBJECT TO
GEOGRAPHICAL DISTRIBUTION

	U-S	D-2	D-1	P-5	P-4	P-3	P-2	P-1	Total	Desirable Range
1962	1	3	13	16	30	25	24	7	119	
1963	1	5	15	13	33	25	15	7	111	98-69
1964	1	3	16	21	31	27	11	4	114	93-66

As more personnel become available from under-represented nations the number of United Kingdom nationals may therefore be expected to fall proportionately. In recent years about two-thirds of the United Kingdom nationals employed in senior UN posts subject to geographical distribution have been based at UN headquarters and a very high percentage of British-held posts are career appointments rather than fixed term, though the gap between the two may be fractionally narrowing rather than widening as indicated in Table B.

---

[26]This grievance was put to Prime Minister Harold Wilson when he met British members of the Secretariat during his visit to the UN on 14 April 1965.

Table B

UNITED KINGDOM STAFF IN PROFESSIONAL AND HIGHER
LEVEL POSTS SUBJECT TO GEOGRAPHICAL DISTRIBUTION

(1) *Career Appointments*

	U-S	D-2	D-1	P-5	P-4	P-3	P-2	P-1	Total
1962	—	3	13	15	23	25	21	6	106
1964	—	3	15	19	27	22	9	4	99

(2) *Fixed-term Appointments*

	U-S	D-2	D-1	P-5	P-4	P-3	P-2	P-1	Total
1962	1	—	—	1	7	—	3	1	13
1964	1	—	1	2	4	5	2	—	5

With respect to posts in the language category, there are normally
about 67 United Kingdom nationals (virtually all of them in career
appointments) in the senior posts as indicated in Table C.

Table C

UNITED KINGDOM NATIONALS IN LANGUAGE POSTS

	1962	*1963*
P-5	3	4
P-4	20	15
P-3	30	34
P-2	13	14
P-1	1	—
Total	67	67

In 1963, the latest year for which overall figures were available, the
total number of United Kingdom nationals employed by the UN was
629; the balance between this figure and the 111 persons in senior
posts subject to geographical distribution and the 67 persons in lan-

guage posts was accounted for by junior posts subject to geographical distribution and posts in the general services.

On occasion the United Kingdom government has been asked to suggest a person for a vacancy at the Under Secretary to D-1 level. When this occurs the matter is likely to come before an interdepartmental committee before the nomination is made, whether the person under discussion is within or outside government service. For senior posts beneath this level such procedure has not been followed: an interested individual puts forward his application to the Secretariat and the government may be completely unaware of his existence, both before and after his appointment by the UN.[27]

The interplay, in terms of appointments, between the United Kingdom civil service and the UN Secretariat is small. A United Kingdom civil servant considering taking a fixed-term contract with the UN has had to ponder the fact that certain difficulties exist about loss of seniority and "getting back on the ladder" upon his return. While it is perhaps arguable that United Kingdom policy should be made more flexible in order to encourage the taking of temporary posts with the UN, a major difficulty to date has been that the diplomatic and foreign service itself has been shortstaffed.

The United Kingdom also provides a large number of technical assistance experts for UN service. In the new Ministry of Overseas Development an International Recruitment Unit[28] seeks to make technical experts available to the UN and its agencies. The UN and UNESCO have generally made good use of the International Recruitment Unit, but international agencies often prefer to act independently when the appointment is very short-term. The WHO makes no use of the International Recruitment Unit and the great majority of FAO experts have been appointed through personal recruitment.

Table D gives some idea of the United Kingdom contribution of technical assistance experts:

(See Table D, Page 54)

---

[27]Though a means of tracing the presence of United Kingdom nationals after an appointment is made is now available through the listing which the Secretary-General submits to the 5th Committee. See, e.g. A/C, 5/L.790 and Add. 1, GAOR, 18th sess.

[28]This was part of the former Department of Technical Cooperation from 1961-4, and from 1949 to 1961 was handled by the Ministry of Labour.

Table D

TECHNICAL ASSISTANCE EXPERTS IN THE FIELD, 1 JANUARY 1965

EXPANDED PROGRAMME OF TECHNICAL ASSISTANCE

	UNTAO	WMO	ITU	ILO	FAO	UNESCO	ICAO	WHO	IAEA	UPU	EPTA TOTAL	REG. PROG.	SPECIAL FUND	OPEX	GRAND TOTAL
United Kingdom	42	4	8	41	76	26	23	45	5	1	271	180	244	10	705
France	40	3	7	64	30	45	4	16	3	1	213	112	161	9	495
China	3	—	—	—	7	—	1	6	—	—	17	10	11	—	38
USSR	4	3	1	—	13	21	2	14	1	—	59	18	24	—	101
United States	34	—	2	14	35	9	9	22	1	—	126	98	140	7	371

Clearly the United Kingdom contributes more nationals to UN field technical assistance posts than any of the five permanent members of the Security Council, including the United States. In January 1965, the grand total of UN technical assistance experts in the field was 4,427, of whom 705 were British; in January 1962, out of a total of 2,289, 375 were British.

The Role of Parliament and the Formulation of United Nations Policy

Parliament's role in the formulation of British policy in the UN is at most marginal. Foreign affairs within the British system of government are executive in character, and the function of Parliament in this respect is to criticize or approve the policies decided upon by the Cabinet. Parliament does not, in any normal sense of the terms, decide upon or conduct foreign policy, but as the constitutional rights of the Government stem from its majority in the House of Commons, it is essential that it maintain the confidence of the House in foreign affairs.

Parliament does have some control over foreign affairs in that it is required to approve each year the Government estimates, which will, within the appropriate sections, contain the United Kingdom contributions to the UN and its specialized agencies. This covers both the assessed share for the particular budgets and voluntary contributions of the United Kingdom to such agencies as EPTA, the Special Fund, or the UN Force in Cyprus. The estimate on these matters will be defended by the minister of the particular department concerned: the Overseas Development Ministry for Special Fund contributions, the Ministry of Aviation for ICAO, and so forth. This control over appropriations is more than counterbalanced by the fact that the conduct of policy through the UN and, indeed, the conduct of foreign affairs generally, usually entails virtually no domestic legislative program, which could be a subject of major debate. Even the ratifying power of Parliament in respect of international treaties, including treaties concluded under UN auspices, is a negative one. Under the Ponsonby rule, treaties concluded by the Government are laid before the House for a period of 21 days and if no objection is made they then attain the force of law. A debate will only take place if the treaty is to have certain internal effects within the United Kingdom.

Other than voting on the estimates, how then does Parliament seek to influence the formulation and presentation of policy in the UN? Members of Parliament are entitled to information from the Government and they may seek it either by oral questions to the minister concerned or by written questions. In 1965 oral questions were put on United Kingdom policy in the UN Special Committee of 33 on Peacekeeping Operations; on the representation of China in the UN; on the briefing of the British delegation to the WHO Assembly; and on the degree to which the United Kingdom was seeking, through the World Bank and FAO, to draw attention to certain store pest and mould fungi. This right to information goes beyond official question time or the practice of written questions, for questions can also be put across the floor of the House during a foreign affairs debate. In addition to the time formally assigned by the government for periodic foreign affairs debates, members may secure the right to an adjournment debate on a topic of their choosing; however, it is virtually unheard of for the UN to be selected as the subject of an adjournment debate. There is also a ballot for motions, and one successful Conservative member used the opportunity in the 1964-65 session to promote a constructive and bipartisan discussion on the UN.

Comparatively few members, however, on either side of the House of Commons, follow UN matters very closely or show any great knowledge in this field. Moreover, there is no standing specialist committee system to encourage such expertise and no foreign relations committee for bipartisan inquiries. Within the Party committees there is equally little tendency towards specialization in UN affairs, or, for that matter, anything else. The Labour Party Foreign Affairs Committee, which all Labour Members are entitled to attend, meets once a week. Sometimes a minister will attend and hear directly the views expressed; on other occasions, a consensus will be reached and conveyed to a minister. The Labour Party Foreign Affairs Committee has a subcommittee on disarmament and another on overseas development. The Conservative Foreign Affairs Committee has no equivalent subcommittees and the UN is a very rare subject for serious discussion. Members of Parliament interested in the UN, therefore, frequently find it preferable to act individually, or in informal groups, rather than through the committees, seeking a minister and influencing his views on a particular aspect of UN policy.

The most organized attempts at influencing policy on UN questions, though still marginal in their effect, occur through two parliamentary inter-party associations:[29] the United Nations Parliamentary Group, which has a membership of 180 members of both houses, and the Parliamentary Group for World Government. Both of these associations, which have a considerable overlap in membership, hold meetings to which experts in UN matters are invited. They may see ministers as well as international civil servants for an exchange

[29]Not to be confused with inter-party committees on particular bills.

of views. The executives of these groups may also draw up memoranda, presenting certain viewpoints on UN policy which are sent to the minister concerned and to the Prime Minister. The Parliamentary Group for World Government has been particularly active in this form of lobbying, with memoranda sent both to the Foreign Secretary and the Prime Minister on such subjects as peacekeeping and UN Charter reform. The aims of the Parliamentary Group for World Government are long-term in character and their position suffers from all the weaknesses of idealism, rarely coming to grips with the major political points at issue. A courteous, but firm response by the Prime Minister is the normal outcome. But matters do at least receive some discussion and this Group has the advantage of a full-time non-parliamentary secretary and an office nearby to provide the various facilities needed by members. The Secretary, as well as the officers of the Committee, are able to go and see people in and out of government in order to obtain a hearing for their views.

The UN Parliamentary Group is content to operate within the framework of the Charter and functions in fairly close concert with the United Nations Association in the United Kingdom, whose secretary for economic and social affairs acts as a clerk to the Parliamentary Group. Unlike the Parliamentary Group for World Government, however, the UN Parliamentary Group, has no paid employee as a secretary.

Pressures for UN Policy Outside of Whitehall and Westminster

As in most countries there are certain institutes and associations outside the formal government and legislative processes that interest themselves either directly in matters or in topics in which the UN itself is involved. They attempt through various channels to present their views to persons who can have a direct influence on the formulations of British policy. The target of the lobbyist is nearly always the minister concerned and comparatively rarely the civil service. The United Nations Association in the United Kingdom tried to obtain general support for, rather than to gain certain objectives for Britain through the UN. There are some 600 local branches of the Association, and they are encouraged, especially at General Election time, to write to their Member of Parliament on UN matters, or to send a deputation to him, or to invite him to address a meeting. The Association has performed valuable services at election times in providing a "neutral platform" on which all the candidates in any one constituency could meet and, after speeches, the audience has had the opportunity to address questions to the candidates on the UN. Local Association branches have encouraged their members to write to candidates asking whether, if elected, they would become members of the United Nations Parliamentary Group.

The Association also lobbies actively on the national level, with leaders of the national executive frequently going as deputations to see ministers, such as the Foreign Secretary, the Minister of State for Disarmament, and the Minister of State for the United Nations, and by maintaining close connections with the Parliamentary Group. Members of the Parliamentary Group, for example, are frequently urged to ask questions in Parliament, either oral or written, on matters, such as the ratification by Britain of the proposals to enlarge ECOSOC and the Security Council, the representation of China, peacekeeping, and so forth.

There exists a Standing Conference on the Economic and Social Work of the United Nations, serviced by the United Nations Association, consisting of some 40 national organizations of international bodies, each of which has a consulative status with ECOSOC. This Standing Conference has four working groups (economic development, refugees, the status of women, and human rights) which meet about four times a year. The Conference has received reports from the British delegate on the Commission of Human Rights and the delegates on the Social Committee, and it has itself submitted names for consideration as the delegate for the Commission on the Status of Women. Before the meeting of its Status of Women Committee, a meeting is usually convened at the House of Commons, to which members of Parliament, officials from the Foreign Office, and senior representatives of women's organizations are invited.

While not exaggerating the influence of the United Nations Association on British attitudes, it is probably fair to say that it plays a role in floating ideas which are sometimes picked up in government circles and in pressing for early action on ideas already accepted in principle, but the Association hardly reflects public opinion strongly enough to bring about reverses in Government policy toward the UN.

Conclusions

The administration of foreign affairs through the UN by the United Kingdom is not as cumbersome or complex as the machinery seems, for the number of persons involved is comparatively small and they are all known to each other. Consultation between individual ministries is facilitated by physical proximity, with one building shared by the Foreign Office and the Commonwealth Relations Office, and by personal friendships, while overall coordination is achieved by a network of inter-ministry committees. The acceptance and implementation of the Plowden Report eradicated many administrative deficiencies that had hampered the effective coordination of the Foreign Office and the Commonwealth Relations Office.

A thorough examination of coordination procedures, however, is impossible for an outsider due to the secrecy that surrounds the system of inter-departmental committees. Although care should be taken not to expose civil servants to undesirable pressures, the lack of scrutiny that this system engenders, even to the extent of not knowing what committees exist, let alone which departments are represented on them, hardly seems in the public interest. The argument that this secrecy is needed in order to portray policy as emanating from the government *as a whole* is not very convincing and the British practice of non-disclosure is at variance with that of France and the United States.

If experience cuts through formal machinery, personality is an attribute which can equally cut through formal hierarchy. A chart of responsibility for UN policy-making shows a somewhat deceptive picture, for it is only part of the tale. Really strong and dynamic ministers inevitably bring to their departments an increased influence. The confidence of certain ministers in particular civil servants, moreover, is a telling factor. An understanding of relations between the United Kingdom and the UN cannot be achieved without appreciating the role of the civil service in British government. Though civil servants serve successive governments and are officially non-partisan, their influence in policy-making is considerable. As in other governmental affairs, finally, the formal machinery may be bypassed in times of crisis and other means of decision-taking may be employed for UN matters.

It is clear that in the last year or two there have been substantive changes in British government machinery that bear directly upon the conduct of foreign policy through the UN. To classify this reorganization as a move towards centralization is to over-simplify. Rather, an endeavor to rationalize the functions of government in certain areas of high priority has perhaps caused a tendency towards centralization so far as UN matters are concerned. It has not been a question of one ministry acquiring a greater degree of authority than before over other ministries, but rather an attempt to locate the ministry where certain aspects of UN policy most logically fall and to give that ministry general, instead of piecemeal, control. Thus, aid functions are now seen as sufficiently important to merit centralizing them in a rather heavily staffed Ministry of Overseas Development and moving them away from control by a tiny staff in the Treasury. At the same time, the Foreign Office retains responsibility for overall policy at the UN as well as co-ordinating the policies promoted through the specialized agencies and there is some evidence that the Foreign Office, with the full support of the Treasury, is seeking to coordinate budgetary policy with regard to the specialized agencies closely with allied countries. The line between supporting the technical work of the specialized agencies and being fully aware of their political implications is a narrow one and time alone will tell if the balance has been correctly struck.

How far the reorganization of British government for UN affairs will last beyond the life of the present Labour government is a matter of conjecture. The reforms stemming from the Plowden Report seem here to stay, but the Conservative party has indicated its opposition to the establishment of the new Ministry of Technology which now handles UN policy in the IAEA, while the Party's intentions concerning the appointment of a Minister of State for Disarmament are unclear. The continued existence under a future Conservative government of the Ministry of Overseas Development seems very likely, but whether it would continue to be headed by a minister of Cabinet rank is an open question.

In the use of "individual experts" on government delegations to the UN or agencies, a contrast may be drawn between the practice of the United Kingdom and that of France. Individuals are, of course, appointed to those posts where genuine freedom from the Government is a stipulated condition, such as the British members of the International Law Commission and of the Committee on Non-Discrimination against Minorities. Individual experts do not participate in normal governmental delegations to UN bodies, much less lead them, although the opinion of individual experts has been sought by many government departments during the policy planning stage.

One weakness in the British system of administering UN affairs is the almost total lack of "feedback." The causes are various. A parliamentarian who goes to New York as part of the delegation to the General Assembly may be expected to learn a great deal and to see matters from a perspective usefully different from that of his foreign service collegues, but little use is made of this experience. There exists no standing foreign relations committee in Parliament to question and cross-examine him, and no report is made to Parliament of his activities or views. Moreover, only the heads of delegations to particular UN committees are required to make reports to the Foreign Office and if a Member of Parliament does not occupy that position he does not report at all to the Foreign Office. Surely improvements could be made. At least a member of Parliament returning from participation in a session of the General Assembly could be required to submit a personal report of his observations and suggestions to the Foreign Office and such a report could be automatically laid in the Library of the House of Commons.

The problem of feedback is apparent in respect of international civil servants also, for the Government believes that British persons serving on the staff of the United Nations should be *bona fide* international servants. In the light of this consideration it is entirely understandable that a person returning from service in the UN Secretariat should not be required to submit any reports, but where his role has been that of a technical assistance expert in the field, the proposition is more arguable. There has been a real lack of information on the worth and efficacy of particular UN programs, and in allocating resources the Treasury and the Ministry of Overseas Development have to a considerable extent been working in the dark. In its responsibility for the ecology of expenditure the Treasury has, in effect, decided on the merits of different projects, yet all too frequently the information required for a rational determination of this sort simply has not been available. Detailed and confidential reports by returning technical assistance experts would obviously help in providing a portion of that information, but it is to the credit of the United Kingdom government that it still believes its first priority must be to promote the concept of an impartial international civil service and to ask for such reports even *after* the completion of an assignment for the UN would not only put this principle in jeopardy, but create problems in respect of any subsequent renewal of employment by the UN.

In any event, the Labour Government elected in 1964 has been anxious that the United Kingdom be seen as a supporter of the UN, and it has with some deliberation directed its policies towards greater assistance for the Organization and its agencies. The decisions to provide logistical support for up to six battalions of UN Forces and to contribute a voluntary $10,000,000 to UN funds during its financial crisis in 1965 may be cited as evidence. During the India-Pakistan fight over Kashmir, moreover, British policy was clearly directed towards strengthening the position of the UN as well as securing a ceasefire, and there have been many firm and unequivocal statements by government ministers of asserting their support for and belief in the economic and social activities of the UN. The cynic may suggest that British support for the UN has occurred only in areas which are not of direct concern to the United Kingdom and that substantial changes in policy have not taken place on such issues as South Africa, Aden, and Southern Rhodesia. Nevertheless, on balance, the United Kingdom seems as ready as any of the world powers today to support the UN in its far-reaching goals and toward that end it has been gradually seeking a better administration of its foreign affairs through the UN system both at home and abroad.

APPENDIX A
List of Abbreviations

ECA	Economic Commission for Africa
ECAFE	Economic Commission for Asia and the Far East
ECE	Economic Commission for Europe
ECLA	Economic Commission for Latin America
ECOSOC	Economic and Social Council
IAEA	International Atomic Energy Agency
IBRD	International Bank for Reconstruction and Development
ICAO	International Civil Aviation Organization
IDA	International Development Association
ILO	International Labour Organization
IMCO	Intergovernmental Maritime Consultative Organization
IMF	International Monetary Fund
ITU	International Telecommunication Union
OECD	Organization for Economic Cooperation and Development
OPEX	Operational Executive and Administrative Personnel Services
UNCTAD	United Nations Conference on Trade and Development
UNEF	United Nations Emergency Force
UNESCO	United Nations Educational, Scientific and Cultural Organization
UNTAD	United Nations Trade and Development
UPU	Universal Postal Union
WHO	World Health Organization
WMO	World Meteorological Organization

APPENDIX B

MEMBERS OF THE SECOND MAXWELL INSTITUTE ON THE UNITED NATIONS

Donald Bishop	Syracuse University
Björn Egge	Norwegian Institute for International Affairs, Oslo
Samaan Farajallah	University of Cairo
Franco Florio	University of Trieste
Pierre Gerbet	National Foundation of Political Science, Paris
Leon Gordenker	Princeton University
Robert Gregg	Syracuse University
H. Field Haviland, Jr.	Brookings Institution, Washington
Rosalyn Higgins	Royal Institute of International Affairs, London
Leo Mates	Institute of International Politics and Economy, Belgrade
Theodor Meron	Israeli Mission to the United Nations
Alvin Rubinstein	University of Pennsylvania
James P. Sewell	Yale University
Jean Siotis	Graduate Institute of International Studies, Geneva
John Stoessinger	City University of New York
Richard Swift	New York University
Roger W. Tubby	U.S. Representative to European Office of the UN
Fernand Van Langenhove	Belgian Institute of International Affairs
Frans A. M. Alting Von Geysau	Tilburg University, Netherlands
Francis O. Wilcox	Johns Hopkins University

Gerard J. Mangone, Director